A Dubious Science

Studies in Modern European History

Frank J. Coppa
General Editor

Vol. 65

PETER LANG
New York • Washington, D.C./Baltimore • Bern
Frankfurt am Main • Berlin • Brussels • Vienna • Oxford

Elizabeth M. Sage

A Dubious Science

Political Economy and the Social Question in 19th-Century France

PETER LANG
New York • Washington, D.C./Baltimore • Bern
Frankfurt am Main • Berlin • Brussels • Vienna • Oxford

Library of Congress Cataloging-in-Publication Data

Sage, Elizabeth M.
A dubious science: political economy and the social question in
19th-century France / Elizabeth M. Sage.
p. cm. — (Studies in modern European history; v. 65)
Includes bibliographical references and index.
1. Economics—France—History—19th century.
2. Economics—Sociological aspects. I. Title.
HB105.A2S24 330.0944'09034–dc22 2009018332
ISBN 978-1-4331-0630-9
ISSN 0893-6897

Bibliographic information published by **Die Deutsche Bibliothek**.
Die Deutsche Bibliothek lists this publication in the "Deutsche
Nationalbibliografie"; detailed bibliographic data is available
on the Internet at http://dnb.ddb.de/.

The paper in this book meets the guidelines for permanence and durability
of the Committee on Production Guidelines for Book Longevity
of the Council of Library Resources.

29 Broadway, 18th floor, New York, NY 10006
www.peterlang.com

Printed in Germany

For sal

Table of Contents

Acknowledgments

This book is the product of many, many years of conversation, research, and writing, and owes its completion to the kind and generous assistance of numerous people.

At the University of Chicago, I am deeply grateful to Jan Goldstein, Leora Auslander, and William Sewell for their sponsorship and support of the original project. At a very early stage in the project, I benefitted from a Council for European Studies predissertation travel grant, as well as from an Eric Cochrane predissertation fellowship. A generous Georges Lurcy Educational Foundation fellowship funded the dissertation research.

In France, I am indebted to the staff at the Académie François Bourdon and the Écomusée du Creusot, in Le Creusot; at the Centre Rhénan d'Archives et de Recherches Économiques and the Archives municipales de Mulhouse, in Mulhouse; at the Archives départementales du Haut-Rhin in Colmar; at the Archives départementales du Saône-et-Loire in Mâcon; at the Archives des houillères de Blanzy in Montceau-les-Mines; and finally, at the Archives nationales and the Bibliothèque nationale in Paris. In particular, I would like to acknowledge the Académie François Bourdon for allowing me to reprint the following materials: "Notice sur la population ouvrière du Creusot," DH/0010, all rights reserved; the Centre Rhénan d'Archives et de Recherches Économiques for allowing me to reprint the following materials: "Prix Salathé," Société Mulhousienne des Cités Ouvrières, A/1425, all rights reserved; and the Archives départementales du Haut-Rhin, for allowing me to reprint the following materials: Mayor of Mulhouse to the Prefect of the Haut-Rhin, 23 February 1829, ADHR 1/M/69; and Hartmann et Compagnie, Malmerspach, to the Juge de Paix of St.-Amarin, 27 May 1853, ADHR 10/M/9, all rights reserved.

At Whittier College, my academic home for the past ten years, I owe thanks to all my friends and colleagues who read pieces of the project, and especially to Laura McEnaney and Bob Marks, for their excellent advice during my moments of self-doubt. Whittier College provided not only several Faculty Research Grants which allowed me to spend time in France, but, more importantly, has provided a friendly, supportive, and collegial environment in which to work, as both an historian and as a teacher of history.

At Peter Lang, I would like to thank Caitlin Lavelle and Nicole Grazioso for their unfailing patience and kind assistance. I thank my parents and my sister for their patience with, and support of, a project that has had a long life.

But finally, and most importantly, I owe my deepest thanks and gratitude to sal johnston, for his willingness to put aside his own work to read mine; for his critical theoretical eye; and for his love, support, and intellectual comradeship, without which this project would never have been completed.

Abbreviations

Académie des sciences morales et politiques	*Académie*
Collège de France	*Collège*
Conservatoire des arts et métiers	*Conservatoire*
École special de commerce de Paris	*École*
Faculté de Droit de Paris	*Faculté*
Journal des économistes	*Journal*
Post-Autistic Economics	PAE
Société des économistes	*Société*

Introduction

This project—a long time in completion—had its origins in a graduate seminar at the University of Chicago on the professionalization of the human sciences in France. In my reading, I came across an intriguing reference to a nineteenth-century French economic journal, the *Journal des économistes.* Surprisingly, the U. of C. library holdings included a full run of this journal, housed on the basement-level of Regenstein Library. I spent months on this floor, sequestered in a corner, a trespasser in the foreign and forbidding realm of economics. Given that I was at the University of Chicago, a bastion of neo-classical economics with its reliance upon complex mathematical models and statistics, what most struck me was the unfamiliarity of the French economics of the mid-nineteenth century, that is, the economics of the *Journal des économistes.* No mathematics; no statistics; a good deal of political commentary; many empirical, almost journalistic, investigations; a rather more dubious science, in other words, than the science that most of the books surrounding me claimed economics to be. I came to realize that its dubious scientificity was in fact the central dynamic and the central dilemma of nineteenth-century French political economy and its practitioners. For nineteenth-century French political economists, the question of whether or not "science" was indeed the correct, and most appropriate, aspiration for economists—the question, in other words, that most late twentieth-century American economists had answered in the affirmative—was still up for grabs.

Oddly enough, as I complete this book, the "scientific" discipline of economics—in Europe, Great Britain, and the United States—is facing challenges from students and faculty who have begun to call for economics to recognize a wider array of approaches to the study of economic circumstances, to rely less upon abstract mathematics, and to focus greater attention on real-life economic situations.[1] It was French students of economics who in 2000 described the neo-classical economics they were being taught as "autistic," that is, cut off from the real world, obsessive, narrow, more concerned with abstract mathematical models than actual economic policy.[2] In an article on the rise of the Post-Autistic Economics movement (or PAE), *Adbusters* quoted a slogan found on a wall on a Madrid university campus (where PAE is increasingly popular): "Economics is about people, not curves."[3] Significantly, this slogan seems to echo the words of many nineteenth-century French economists who also decried what they understood to be an unfortunate and dangerous disregard of real people and real situations in favor of supposedly scientific laws and theories. While the PAE slogan is certainly catchier, a quick glance at a statement written by political economist Théodore Fix in an 1845 *Journal des économistes* article suggests the historical familiarity of PAE's sentiment:

> Without a doubt, political economy, considered in the most restrained and strict sense of the word, is nothing but the science of the production of wealth....But when the practical consequences and results of its [formulas and laws] are examined, one encounters man facing you, man with his needs, tendencies and passions. Thus, political economy is no longer this simple science that unfolds in an inflexible manner in a series of axioms and propositions. It finds itself grappling with the most diverse interests, with social necessities, with morality, with politics, even with the difference of conditions and intelligence, and finally with institutions, practices and traditions.[4]

This resurrection of the nineteenth-century predecessors of contemporary French economics actually serves to bear out one of PAE's central complaints about economics: its marginalization of history.[5] Had history—not just as an analytical method but as a narrative of the discipline's own past—not been relegated to the outer reaches of the economic discipline, the students who make up the bulk of the PAE movement would have seen their own economic predecessors practicing an economics that looked very much like what they want for themselves. In fact, the question of whether there is room within the study of economic phenomena for historical methods has historical antecedents. Nineteenth-century French economists regularly asked themselves what the inclusion of history might do to the presumed scientificity of political economy.

Simply put, the French discipline of economics has a history, one that has been easy to forget once mathematics rather than history became the discipline's benchmark. Probably unbeknownst to themselves, French students advocating for greater attention to people rather than curves are following quite closely in the footsteps of their nineteenth-century predecessors, revisiting some of the same debates, and confronting some of the same issues. What Post-Autistics Economics demonstrates—at least to the academic historian of French political economy—is the history of disciplinary change, of rethinking old disciplinary assumptions and pushing old disciplines in new directions. The questions and demands of Post-Autistic Economics in France evoke images of nineteenth-century French political economists asking whether political economy was actually a science; how it might be a different science than physics, mathematics, or chemistry; and how political economy's examination of people and human interactions (rather than, say, planetary motion or chemical reactions) might render it a more vague, imprecise, and ambiguous science–in short, a more dubious science–than physics, mathematics, or chemistry. What it might mean to call contemporary economics a "dubious science" is a question I will leave to others; what it meant for nineteenth-century political economists is the story this project purports to tell.

This book narrates a history of the dubious science of political economy and its struggle to achieve scientific legitimacy and academic status.[6] My discussion of this dubious science spans the period from the late eighteenth century when French economists first considered themselves to be practitioners of a science with its own universal laws, to the early twentieth century when the French welfare state assumed responsibility for many of the social problems that political economy had considered its natural terrain. More specifically, this book chronicles political economists' mid-nineteenth-century encounter with "the social question," or *la question sociale,* and the disciplinary dilemma that *la question sociale* posed for them. *La question sociale,* which referred collectively to everything from working-class poverty to workplace indiscipline to unionization, strikes, and working-class socialist activism, represented a significant challenge for nineteenth-century French political economists. It offered concrete evidence that economists' theoretical assumptions were not working in practice the way they were supposed to, and that industrial capitalism was showing little sign of guaranteeing happiness and economic success to all productive members of society. *La question sociale* demonstrated that *laissez-faire* was not proving the best way to solve problems of social misery, and gave rise to the interventionist strategy of industrial paternalism, exercised on behalf of workers by their employers, as a better solution to the collective problems of the French working class. In short, *la question sociale* jeopardized economists' claims to have uncovered and understood the scientific laws that regulated the economy and people's interactions within that economy. *La question sociale* thus threatened the scientific legitimacy that political economists coveted, and forced them to devise strategies to protect their discipline's theoretical foundations, its claims to scientific authority, and its academic positions and opportunities.

These protective strategies took the form of an odd category, known as *économie sociale,* or social economy, that was created by political economy and that operated both alongside and outside it. As a poorly-defined, eminently flexible category, social economy provided a protective border around political economy; as the category that held everything that did not comfortably fit into the narrowly-defined science of political economy, namely *la question sociale,* social economy offered political economy the opportunity, the site, and the justification to participate in discussions of social misery and social antagonism. Because social economy was technically something other than political economy, political economists could remain true to their original theoretical tenets, continue to define their discipline as a science, and continue to demand institutional legitimacy on the grounds of its scientific authority. But while in the short run social economy allowed economists to achieve the legitimacy they so longed for, in the long run it escaped economists' authority. If economists invented *économie sociale* as a place to hide *la question sociale* and what it implied about the need for government of the population and regulation of industrial capitalism, they eventually lost control of their invention, accidentally launching into public discourse a way of thinking and talking about *la question sociale* that undermined the basic tenets of their science.

The disciplinary dilemmas of nineteenth-century French political economy might at first glance appear to offer little of interest to those outside the field of economic thought and its history. Political economists' efforts to protect their discipline from the challenge of *la question sociale* took the form of often Byzantine discussions and debates: over what exactly *la question sociale* meant for their science, what exactly social economy was, how to properly label and define both political economy and social economy, and how to set social economy's boundaries vis-à-vis political economy. Far from being dry and obscure academic debates, however, economists' discussions of *la question sociale* and its disciplinary implications offer insight not only into the social realities of an industrializing society, but also into the manner in which all academic disciplines, not just nineteenth-century political economy, work; the way their assumptions and basic premises alter; the way those alterations are determined and constrained by disciplines' "tactical considerations,"[7] that is, by what they want, the circumstances to which they are responding, and the manner in which they try to protect themselves; and the unintended, surprising, and often unwanted consequences of these tactical considerations. This project, then, uses the history of nineteenth-century

French political economy to explore the relationship between the material realities of nineteenth-century France and the processes of disciplinary formation, transformation, and self-protection. Furthermore, the history of political economy offers a case study of a *human* science, and thus of political economists' century-long struggle with the implications of studying people rather than curves. Political economy is another example of a human science—alongside the more familiar examples of medicine, psychiatry, social work, and criminology—struggling with the social consequences of nineteenth-century industrialization and urbanization.

Political economy also offers a promising site from which to explore the interrelationship between the multiple meanings of the term "discipline": a type of power and the techniques used to exercise that power; a branch of knowledge; and a social entity, for instance, a profession or an institution.[8] Economists were engaged in the creation of a legitimate branch of knowledge, the "science" of economics, and were committed to creating an authoritative academic discipline, and to securing an institutional position and status for their discipline. But through their efforts to promote a paternalist solution to *la question sociale*, economists were also implicated in the identification of solutions to combat problems of discipline. For French industrialists, the social question posed both a problem *of* discipline—how were workers to be disciplined into being productive and obedient at work, and moral, thrifty, law-abiding, and temperate at home—as well as a problem *for* the emergent discipline of political economy and for its disciplinary aspirations.

Finally, economists' struggle with *la question sociale* and its implications links the history of the discipline of nineteenth-century French political economy to the broader subject of governmentality, that peculiarly modern type of power explored by Michel Foucault which takes the form of extra-state administered strategies and programs designed to collect information about both populations and individuals in order to better manage, control and reconfigure them. People, according to French political economists, were resources of the state, and in economists' concern with *la question sociale*, one senses not only a recognition of what might happen to individual workers should their miseries be ignored, but also an awareness that miserable, sick, underfed people could not contribute effectively to the wealth and strength of a state. By the end of the nineteenth century, French political economy, like other human sciences, had been unintentionally and unexpectedly embroiled in a network of interventionist strategies, administered both from inside and outside the state, designed to produce docile bodies, obedient souls, and a content and productive population.

One could legitimately describe this project as a genealogy, a term that immediately (and correctly) suggests a Foucauldian inspiration. Foucault once described genealogy as the project of liberating "subjugated knowledges," forms of knowledge that have been disqualified, excluded, or de-legitimized in the pursuit of scientific status and thus power.[9] In a lecture at the *Collège de France*, Foucault declared:

> "...we should be asking the question, asking ourselves about the aspiration to power that is inherent in the claim to being a science. The question or questions that have to be asked are: 'What types of knowledge are you trying to disqualify when you say that you are a science? What speaking subject, what discursive subject, what subject of experience and knowledge are you trying to minorize when you begin to say: "I speak this discourse, I am speaking a scientific discourse, and I am a scientist." What theoretico-political vanguard are you trying to put on the throne in order to detach it from all the massive, circulating, and discontinuous forms that knowledge can take?'"[10]

Foucault's questions are all, in fact, particularly suitable and instructive ones for the self-titled science of political economy. Political economy during the nineteenth century strove for scientific status and power, and attempted to protect itself from unwanted knowledge—all that knowledge represented by the phrase *la question sociale*—that appeared to invalidate its claims to be a science. In this process of protecting itself, political economy elevated particular types of knowledge and disqualified others; it narrowed particular avenues of inquiry and widened others. In the history of French political economy, then, social economy was a disqualified knowledge, an inferior knowledge that was, in fact, given an inferior position vis-à-vis political economy. Whereas political economy never completely dismissed knowledge of the social question—the knowledge embodied in social economy—political economy nonetheless corralled that knowledge, keeping it close but not too close, in such a way that its challenge to political economy could be neutralized. In short, engaging in a genealogical investigation of political economy does exactly what Foucault intended a genealogy to do, that is, make the operations of power—usually invisible—visible, and uncover the strategizing and maneuvering behind any academic discipline's pretensions to truth.

The voices that speak the loudest in this book are those of nineteenth-century political economists. Theirs was an intellectual engagement with the industrial world of nineteenth-century France; they examined French industrial society from their desks and meeting rooms in Paris. Their encounter with *la question sociale* and their efforts to deflect its challenge to their discipline occurred in the pages of their own writing: essays in the pages of economic journals; investigations of working-class towns, labor conditions, and lives; on-going debates and discussions among economists that spanned both volumes and years. The voices of the central figures in the field of French political economy emerge, then, from their own periodicals, especially the *Journal des économistes*, the principal organ of nineteenth-century French political economy and the most influential of French economic periodicals, as well as from their own published books and pamphlets.

Softer are the voices of French industrialists, who most directly experienced the industrialization process and *la question sociale*. It was industrialists who offered the descriptions of *la question sociale* and proposals for its solution that economists in turn studied, promoted and grafted onto their science. Softest, finally, are the voices of French workers themselves, seen in this book through the eyes of French political economists who encountered them as raw data, but as raw data with weighty significance not only for the scientific aspirations of political economy, but for the health and stability of French society.[11]

My investigation begins in the early nineteenth century, a period in which the principal goal of the discipline of political economy was to promote itself as a socially-useful science, based upon its comprehension of certain universal and natural laws. Chapter One examines the abstract knowledge that economists believed they controlled; the particular problems over which economists believed they had jurisdiction; the men economists claimed as their founders and champions; and the rewards they claimed for the recognition of their jurisdictional claims. Chapter Two explores the mid-nineteenth century encounter between French political economy and *la question sociale*, and economists' confrontation with real empirical data that challenged, if not invalidated, their scientific assertions, and refuted their claims to be the practitioners of a socially beneficial discipline. Chapter Three investigates political economists' efforts to solve both the intellectual and institutional problems caused for their science by their encounter with the unexpected *la question sociale*. This chapter analyzes the odd category of *économie sociale*, which began to appear in economists' writing at the same time as their encounter with *la question sociale*, and which offered economists a means of grafting *la question sociale* onto political economy, thus protecting its scientific pretensions and their professional ambitions. Finally, Chapter

Four narrates political economists' failure to control the meaning and use of the category of *économie sociale*. By the end of the nineteenth century, social economy had been launched into the public sphere as a discourse that not only proliferated beyond economists' ability to control it, but that signaled the obsolescence of economists' traditional understanding of their science.

1. A Promising Science: Political Economy Before 1840

In 1840, French political economists had reason to feel simultaneously hopeful and discouraged about the state of the science of political economy and their status as professional advocates and practitioners of that new science. The period before 1840 had seen the strengthening of the basic tenets of political economy and a growing consensus as to its underlying and indisputable foundations. It was a period in which economists attempted to forge a legitimacy for themselves and their science, and to publicize their scientific tenets for the good, they argued, of France's social harmony and economic well-being. It was during this period that a variety of political economic journals were launched, and the first chairs of economic science founded. The outlook appeared, then, promising.

On the other hand, early nineteenth-century French political economists also acknowledged that theirs was still not a popular science. Political economy's association with the Enlightenment tradition, liberal philosophy, and anti-clericalism had made it an object of suspicion under Napoleon and the Restoration monarchy, forcing economists to take precautions, both intellectual and practical. While political economists would welcome the constitutional July Monarchy in 1830 as assuring them a more favorable political environment in which to practice and publicize their science, by 1840 economists had still not achieved the status they desired for themselves and their science, and their sense of having been slighted (as the "dismal science"[1]), not only by popular opinion but also by the state that controlled higher education and academic appointments, was palpable. In 1840 most economists still operated outside the academic sphere proper, forming private political economy clubs and self-financing the publication of their writings. Those who did teach often held posts in private technical schools, or taught not as professors of political economy, but of engineering or of commerce. Thus, while the situation of political economy was rosier in 1840 than it had been in 1815, economists were certain that there was much to do before their science could be described as having achieved its rightful professional position and status.

"Professions are," to quote sociologist Andrew Abbott, "exclusive occupational groups applying somewhat abstract knowledge to particular cases."[2] But a profession is only a profession if and when it is recognized *as* a profession. Recognition is crucial, and is usually sought by an aspiring profession through a jurisdictional claim, that is, a request by a profession to someone or something in search of authority and rights: the authority to analyze, diagnose, and treat a particular problem; the right to be paid appropriately for that work; the right to control access to a body of abstract knowledge. As Abbott states, "public jurisdiction, in short, is a claim of both social and cultural authority."[3]

This chapter is all about one particular jurisdictional claim: the claim by political economy to be a certain science that observed the natural workings of the economy. This chapter will explore French political economy both as a body of knowledge—and significantly, as a *scientific* body of knowledge—and as an aspiring academic profession that promoted particular jurisdictional claims during the first half of the nineteenth century. In France, where the state had traditionally held the power to grant and withdraw professional rights and professional authority, professional jurisdictional claims were usually made to the State, or to elements within the State.[4] During the nineteenth century, political economists sought to have their jurisdictional claims legitimized and their expertise recognized by the Ministry of Public Instruction, and those claims embodied in professional posts within the system of higher education. And thus, much of the work of nineteenth-century French economists consisted of using the university posts they had won, along with other professional organizations, as sites for continued disciplinary self-promotion.

The chapter first investigates the central theoretical foundations of this presumably universal and natural science as they were understood by political economists, as well as the social implications of those foundations, particularly for the working majority of the population. It then examines how French economists of the early nineteenth century understood the founding texts of their science, as well as how they understood the founders of that science, namely Adam Smith and Jean-Baptiste Say. The third part of the chapter describes the diverse practitioners of French political economy in the first decades of the nineteenth century, as well as the professional posts within higher education that economists had secured as a result of their jurisdictional claims, and explores how those posts, as well as other strongholds of the profession, functioned as sites of further self-promotion on behalf of the new science.

By 1840, the science of political economy benefitted from several important academic posts, a body of practitioners confident in their scientific authority and anxious to gain professional status, and the support of a relatively sympathetic state. A year later, in 1841, political economists would found a journal, the *Journal des économistes*, which would prove a key site of self-promotion for the science, and would continue to be the most influential economic journal in France throughout the nineteenth century. And yet, if there was cause for cautious celebration among French political economists in 1840, there were also disquieting signs that their science faced challenges that they had never considered, doubts and anxieties among their own colleagues, and broad social fears about the consequences—physical, economic, and moral—of the industrial capitalism that French economists so eagerly promoted. Precisely at the moment of their utmost confidence in the certain theoretical principles and beneficial consequences of their science, French political economists were confronted with real empirical data that challenged, if not invalidated, the assertions of their science, and that refuted economists' claims to be the practitioners of a socially beneficial discipline.

The Confident Scientific Tenets of Political Economy

Political economists' surprise by mid-century that their science might not be operating in practice the way it was theoretically supposed to, derived from their understanding of what political economy was: a universal science with precise, unambiguous, and invariable principles. French political economists in the 1830s and 1840s were notable for their firm belief in the science of political economy, and for their conviction that theirs was an abstract and theoretical science akin to physics. Theirs was also a science with a history, a science with masters. Writing about political economy in the pages of the *Journal des économistes* or teaching a course in political economy at the *Conservatoire des arts et métiers* was, for French economists, to work within a hallowed tradition. Economists were aware of—and relied upon—their history; they were resolutely committed to the laws of their science; and thus any discussion of nineteenth-century French political economy needs to begin with that science, that history, and those masters.

Central to the foundations of early nineteenth-century French political economy was the notion that a natural order, created by God for the happiness of human beings, existed in the world.[5] This natural order was regulated by universal laws applicable to all societies. Unfortunately, this natural order and its laws had been obscured by the artificial creations of human society, and thus could be revealed only by stripping away the artifice created by centuries of human tradition and ignorance. Once the natural order had been revealed, and its laws understood, societies could begin to conform to them.

The science of political economy was understood by French economists as the study of the natural laws governing the economy and wealth.[6] The central "universal law" for political economy was the self-regulating mechanism of the market economy. Prices, wages, the supply of and demand for goods: all were determined by economic laws that tended toward equilibrium. According to economists, the natural state of the economy was a stable and balanced condition. Economic crises and instabilities were merely temporary readjustments effected by the economy itself. The epitome of this self-regulating mechanism was the law of supply and demand. Simply put, when the supply of a particular good exceeded its demand, its price decreased; when the demand for a particular good exceeded its supply, its price increased. Similarly, when the supply of labor exceeded its demand, wages decreased; when the demand for labor exceeded its supply, wages increased.[7] According to economists, artificial attempts to control these self-regulating mechanisms—for instance, by demanding wages higher than the market dictated, or by forcing wages below market-levels—were never successful, and only destabilized the economy.

Given that the economy was understood to be a natural phenomenon, operating according to universal, self-regulating, and balanced laws, the best approach to the economy, and to economic affairs, was thought to be a hands-off (*laissez-faire*) stance.[8] Detectable problems with the French economy—whether unemployment, social misery, high taxes, high prices, or low wages—were due, political economists argued, to the fact that the French state had not yet divested itself of protectionist and interventionist policies, and that people, workers in particular, had not yet embraced their inviolable right to self-determination, or acknowledged the duty of self-responsibility this right dictated.

Early nineteenth-century economists argued that both reason and liberty were inherent in human nature. Unique to human beings was the ability to use reason in order to progress both intellectually and morally.[9] With reason, one's ability to exercise natural human liberty and to accept responsibility for oneself also increased.[10] The individual's right to self-determination was thus an inviolable right; each individual had the right to make his/her own decisions, determine his/her course of action, and surmount obstacles by him/herself. For political economists, the right of individual self-determination meant first and foremost the right to determine the use of one's own labor. An individual's labor power was private property, and consequently, each individual had the right to dispose of that private property as he or she deemed fit. Political economists distrusted any attempt to regulate an individual's labor by setting limits on the workday, restricting certain types of employment to certain types of people, or creating minimum wages.

The right of individual self-determination also implied the duty of accepting responsibility for the results of one's decisions. If individuals had the right to live and work, they also had to recognize that they, and they alone, bore the responsibility for the outcome of their decisions about how they wanted to live and work.[11] The duty of self-responsibility, economists argued, had the added benefit of allowing people to understand the consequences of their actions. If people were never encouraged to assume responsibility for their actions, and hence to experience the consequences, good or bad, of these actions, they would have no means of learning which actions were beneficial and which were harmful. As Frédéric Bastiat wrote in 1851:

> But for experience to be a lesson, for it to fulfill its mission in the world, for it to develop foresight, for it to expose a series of effects, for it to provoke good habits and restrain bad ones; in a word, for it to be the necessary instrument of progress and moral perfection, it is necessary that the law of responsibility functions. It is necessary that unfortunate consequences are felt, and, let's use the fatal word, it is necessary that evil temporarily holds sway.[12]

This inviolable right of individual self-determination was the source of the economic prescription *laissez-faire, laissez-passer*. Political economists were troubled by artificial constraints placed on the individual, and by government superseding of individual initiative.[13] Since they believed individuals to be perfectly capable of exercising responsibility for their actions, and since the natural order was supposedly self-regulating, outside intervention was perceived either as tyrannical, or as disrupting the natural regulatory mechanisms of the social order. Their commitment to what they called "liberty" made economists fervent anti-protectionists and anti-interventionists.[14] For political economists, *laissez-faire, laissez-passer* denoted an economy free of state regulation and protection, in which free trade and free competition were allowed to flourish. Government participation was needed only to assure social order, justice, and private property; it was unnecessary in the process of economic growth.[15] Economic prosperity was best left to the natural self-regulation of the economy and to individuals' natural right of self-determination.

At the root of the natural order lay the compatibility between individual self-interest and the public well-being. Self-interest was assumed to be an essential human psychological trait that was both good and just since it had been created by God. The pursuit of self-interest, therefore, was fully in keeping with the goal of social happiness. This is not to say that every human action motivated by self-interest was undertaken with one eye to the public interest. Instead, the mechanism of the "invisible hand," elaborated in Adam Smith's *The Wealth of Nations*, ensured that actions undertaken out of self-interest would naturally satisfy both the needs of the individual and the needs of society. Since a natural harmony of interests existed between the individual and common interest, individuals could be left alone to exercise their right of self-determination without threat of social disruption. In French economists' view, the pursuit of an individual's economic self-interest posed no threat to social happiness. They argued that capitalism, the division of labor, free trade, and competition, all of which were grounded in the pursuit of economic self-interest, would assure prosperity and happiness for everyone.

Underlying this argument was the basic assumption that all people had the same basic interests.[16] The economic world was the product of actions undertaken by all members of society; since all types of work and all types of workers created wealth, all types of work and all social classes were equally indispensable for economic prosperity.[17] In his *Traité d'économie politique*, published in 1803, Jean-Baptiste Say recognized only one social division capable of splintering society: the distinction between producers and non-producers, the latter composed of government officials, clergymen, and military officers. While the interests of the producing and non-producing classes differed radically, interests within the producing class itself were assumed by Say to remain the same. As some have noted, Say seems never to have perceived a division of the producing class into two competing classes, the laboring and the employing classes, each with very different interests.[18]

As self-proclaimed scientists of the natural laws governing the economy and wealth, economists assumed that the producers of wealth—and in particular, the laboring classes—fell under their umbrella of professional expertise. According to that expertise, workers were free individuals, blessed with reason, and hence capable of making their own decisions, determining their own behaviors, and improving their material conditions by themselves. Workers possessed the "right to labor," the freedom to choose for whom they worked, how long and often they worked, and what they were willing to accept as payment. A wage contract was deemed to control the relationship between workers and their employers. The wage contract was a mutually binding contract, negotiated between two free and equal individuals, each of whom could reject the conditions of the contract. If the proposed wages seemed insufficient to workers, they were free to offer their labor power elsewhere. Similarly, if the proposed wages were prohibitively high for employers, they were free to refuse to hire workers.[19] According to political economic theory, the wage levels proposed in a wage contract under negotiation were not arbitrarily set by employers and workers, but instead were the result of the natural fluctuations of the supply and demand of labor power, and hence, of the price of labor. Since wages were determined by the natural self-regulating mechanism of supply and demand, any attempts to artificially set wages ran the risk of destabilizing the entire market. Strikes and coalitions were two standard methods of attempting to artificially control the price of labor, and both, economists argued, were dangerous mistakes.[20]

Since political economists assumed the economic organization of society to be natural, balanced, and thus by definition good and just, and all individuals to be free, equal, and endowed with reason, any problems experienced by French workers were deemed the result of the improper exercise of their right of self-determination and the insufficient shouldering of their duty of self-responsibility. The most prominent proponent of the argument that workers' misery was their own fault was political economist Charles Dunoyer. He pointed out that the bourgeoisie itself had emerged from the medieval working class, and had managed to ascend the social ladder because of hard work, thrift, and morality.[21] If the nineteenth-century working class was unable to pull itself up the social ladder as the bourgeoisie had once done, it was due to lack of effort, immorality, and ignorance rather than to a *laissez-faire* economic system. Economists like Dunoyer regularly pointed out that workers were miserable because they immediately spent all their money rather than putting it aside for an uncertain future, spent too much time in the *café* and not enough time in the workshop, and married young and "multiplied with a bestial fecundity...."[22]

As workers' misery was their own fault, economists argued, government had no obligation to take care of working-class problems that resulted from improvidence and immorality. Before 1840, then, most political economists condemned all forms of organized state assistance to workers.[23] Workers needed to learn that their actions and behaviors had consequences, and that they must develop the qualities with which they could improve their material conditions. State aid to workers would only convince them that the state would protect them, thereby encouraging further laziness, immorality, and improvidence. Furthermore, state assistance would infringe upon the inviolability of the economic sphere by artificially setting wages, controlling the food supply, and interfering with workers' right to labor and industrialists' right to control their labor force. In short, state assistance would nullify the individual's rights of self-determination and self-responsibility.[24] According to economists Théodore Fix and Joseph Garnier, the only legitimate remedies for working-class misery were those that did not interfere in the way that society and the economy were organized. Fix argued that encouraging religion, hard work, and sobriety among workers were all good solutions to the problem of misery.[25] Garnier also suggested that workers be taught basic economic principles so that they would learn how to succeed in a *laissez-faire*, capitalist economy.[26]

Unlike economists' vociferous opposition to the question of state assistance, however, the practice of charity was approached with unmistakable ambivalence. Charity was a natural human sentiment, economists acknowledged, and there were times when moral duties dictated that the unfortunate be helped. The problem with state-sponsored charity, however, was that it encouraged workers to assume (erroneously) that charity was a positive right, something owed to them. Economists pointed out that legal charity also destroyed the personal impulse to be charitable, and made the rich resent rather than pity the poor.[27] Furthermore, even private charity entailed risks. Private efforts could, variously, spoil or degrade workers, encourage laziness and immorality, or destroy their self-respect. Economists argued, therefore, that charity could only temporarily relieve misery and could never completely compensate for laziness, immorality or improvidence. In short, political economy taught that as a rule the best solution to working-class misery was to do nothing. Neither state assistance nor charity could do what the practice of *laissez-faire* could: teach workers that their misery and its relief was their own burden. An often harsh reality, economists admitted, but a reality nonetheless.

The Masters of the Science and their Fictional Selves

For the French political economists of the early nineteenth century espousing the above precepts, the founder of their science was Adam Smith, who had elaborated the basic tenets of political economy in his 1776 masterpiece, *An Inquiry into the Nature and Causes of the Wealth of Nations.* Political economists in nineteenth-century France traced their origins back to Smith and what they understood to be his unmistakable and inflexible insistence upon the principle of *laissez-faire.*[28] The other economist to whom they were indebted was the French political economist Jean-Baptiste Say, who had clarified and systematized the rather unwieldy ideas elaborated in Smith's *The Wealth of Nations,* and popularized Smith's scientific tenets in France.[29] For French political economists writing before 1840, the most significant of Say's accomplishments was his emphasis on the scientific nature of political economy. It was Say who had supposedly applied the scientific methods of the hard sciences to political economy, transforming political economy into an abstract and theoretical science that emulated the hard sciences of physics and chemistry.[30] He had done in France, in other words, what David Ricardo had done for the science of political economy in Great Britain, that is, render it a "rigorous discipline offering conclusions as certain as those offered by Euclidean geometry."[31] The exact sciences, with their natural laws, their experimental methods, their mathematical simplicity and precision, were what all new bodies of knowledge in the nineteenth century sought to emulate. As historians Joyce Appleby, Lynn Hunt, and Margaret Jacob have written:

> natural science with its experimental method came in the eighteenth century to be seen as the measure of all human truth. Imitate mechanical science, follow its methods, seek laws for everything from human biology to the art of governing – that was the advice bequeathed to the Western world by the Enlightenment.[32]

Appleby et al. refer to this as the "heroic model of science," a term that French economists would have themselves appreciated. The science of political economy proposed to heroically liberate individuals from unnatural constraints upon their self-interest, their free choice, and their self-responsibility. It *was* heroic, in the minds of French economists, to espouse a "system of natural liberty," as Smith referred to it, and to emancipate the individual from arbitrary government restrictions.[33]

Early nineteenth-century political economists, then, following what they believed to have been Say's lead, viewed political economy as a hard science, despite their lack of a mathematical and/or statistical method. It was the observation of general, recurring phenomena, not calculation, and thus the discovery of the laws which regulated the economic sphere, that characterized the science of political economy and that, in fact, had led to the realization that political economy *was* a science. According to early nineteenth-century French economists, it was Say's presumed emphasis upon the abstract and theoretical nature of political economy that distinguished him from Adam Smith. French economists believed that Adam Smith had viewed the economy as an organic, living and breathing social body, and the economist as a doctor, giving advice and thus healing, rather than a scientist who simply studied and diagnosed. But while they were correct in identifying Say's distaste for the idea of the scientist offering advice—after all, physicists did not give advice about planetary motion or the properties of gravity—they were too hasty in their portrayal of Say as a consistent believer in the abstract, universal, impartial, analytic, and scientific properties of political economy.[34] Say himself seems never to have been either as certain or as consistent about the type of science political economy was, as his followers presumed him to have been. In his *Cour complet d'économie politique*, published in 1828, four years prior to his death, Say described, in terms that evoked Smith, the social body as a living thing, and political economy as the study of that living thing:

> The study that has been done of nature and the functions of the human body has created a body of ideas, a science which has been given the name of "physiology." The study of the nature and the functions of the social body has also created a science: political economy, or better, social economy [*l'économie politique, ou mieux, sociale*].[35]

This gap—between the certainty of Say's followers as to the type of science Say believed political economy to be, and the doubts and reconsiderations of Say himself—provides an interesting example of what historians of economic thought have long pointed to as the misreading of both Smith and Say by the generation of economists who followed them.

For the French political economists of the early nineteenth century, Adam Smith and Jean-Baptiste Say had given a mature shape to the science that explained the natural, self-regulating laws of the production, consumption and distribution of wealth. Before 1840, most French economists were confident that they understood what both Smith and Say had intended for the science of political economy, and were certain that the tenets they themselves espoused—and most significantly the principle of *laissez-faire*—were those that Smith and

Say had as well. And yet, some economic historians have argued that the Adam Smith and Jean-Baptiste Say who French economists acknowledged as architects of their science were partial fictions and historical myths. It is not surprising, then, that economic historians have referred both to "the Adam Smith Problem" and "the Jean-Baptiste Say Problem," the problem, in other words, of distinguishing between what Smith and Say actually intended—for their science; by precepts like *laissez-faire*; or by the policy of state non-intervention—and how the two men's ideas came to be understood (or misunderstood) by those who followed them. For the disciplinary transformations in which French economists would have to engage after 1840, these fictional Adam Smiths and Jean-Baptiste Says were crucial, insofar as they structured the science of political economy that economists confronted. When mid-century French economists were faced with evidence suggesting that theirs was not an exact and inflexible science like physics, but rather a messy and dubious one, rethinking the basic structures and implications of their science would entail rethinking the particular Adam Smiths and Jean-Baptiste Says who they had invented, relied upon, and would now have to reinterpret.

Although French political economists were certain that Adam Smith had advocated *laissez-faire, laissez-passer* as a fundamental and dogmatic principle, historians of Smith's thought have been less certain. While Smith had certainly believed that governments had a tendency to meddle where they were not needed, and that reliance upon the market offered a more assured policy for promoting the general welfare of a population, he also understood that government action was sometimes necessary, precisely in order to promote the same general welfare of the population. The famous and much-cited chapter in *The Wealth of Nations* describing the effects of the division of labor on the creativity and intelligence of workers—the monotony of engaging in the same task hour after hour, day after day—was followed by Smith's warning that it was only by government action, specifically in the form of public education for those same workers, that their intellectual decline could be prevented.[36] Economic historian Roger Backhouse argues that Smith's system of natural liberty—"the freedom of any individual to bring his capital into competition with that of any other man"[37]—depended upon national defense, a system of justice, public institutions (such as education), and public works (well-maintained roads, canals, and bridges). It was government that provided these public benefits without which natural liberty would have been impossible.[38] Adam Smith understood, then, that there were important exceptions to the principle of *laissez-faire*, particularly when the welfare of the poor was at stake. Despite being interpreted by later generations of economists as a proponent of, and apologist for, the manufacturing class, Smith was frequently critical of the "mean rapacity, the monopolizing spirit of the merchants and manufacturers."[39] Instead of the much-touted "harmony of interests," Smith recognized that the interests of workers and employers, as well as their respective bargaining positions, were not always identical in practice:

> What are the common wages of labour, depends everywhere upon the contract usually made between those two parties, whose interests are by no means the same. The workmen desire to get as much, the masters to give as little as possible. The former are disposed to combine in order to raise, the latter in order to lower the wage of labor.[40]

Smith also recognized that masters always had the advantage in negotiating wage contracts or wage disputes, since they were able to hold out longer against workers' demands.[41]

And yet despite all this ambivalence vis-à-vis the role of government, the division of labor, the manufacturing classes, and the harmony of interests, Smith was understood by many of his successors to be a strict proponent of *laissez-faire*, and an unswerving supporter of the capitalist manufacturing class. Smith's carefully nuanced and limited demand that government not meddle in the market when it did not need to was distorted into a dogmatic critique of governmental intervention, no matter where it appeared or for what purposes. As Emma Rothschild points out, Smith "has come to epitomize the one-sided, reductionist enlightenment of *laissez-faire* economics."[42]

The same fate—to have been misunderstood by his successors and reduced to a one-sided caricature of himself—awaited Jean-Baptiste Say as well. After his death in 1832, and largely due to the interpretation of his work by his son Horace Say, Jean-Baptiste Say came to be known in France as an orthodox classical political economist of the liberal school, and thus as a proponent of *laissez-faire* and governmental non-interference. There were, however, other ways to have interpreted Say's work; historian Richard Whatmore, in his work on Say, cites Charles Comte, Say's son-in-law, who understood Say to have been *not* a liberal, but first and foremost a proponent of republicanism.[43] And yet, it was Horace Say's understanding of his father's ideas and intentions that dominated, and hence the Jean-Baptiste Say of orthodox *laissez faire* opinions, who was handed down to succeeding generations of French political economists. Making matters even more complicated, this fictional Say was actually a double fiction. If Say was understood (incorrectly) by his son to have been a follower of Adam Smith, it was a fictional Adam Smith who Say was understood to have followed and popularized: the unambiguously pro-*laissez faire* and anti-interventionist Adam Smith.[44] These complicated fictions would make the job of later French political economists, anxious to re-think their science and to untangle some of these intellectual snarls, exceedingly difficult and convoluted.

Richard Whatmore has reexamined the political economy of Say to reveal both a committed republican, and an unorthodox political economist, someone whose ideas were claimed by his friend Simonde de Sismondi as having more in common with his own than with the classical political economists of Great Britain, David Ricardo and Thomas Malthus.[45] Throughout his life, Say believed that republicanism was compatible with a large, commercial society like France.[46] For its success and stability, a fully commercial, republican society needed people imbued with both public and private virtues and with simple tastes, who had the opportunity to create comfortable lives and moderate wealth for themselves. Political economy was, then, the subject that explained how this moderate wealth could be created within the modern republican state, and what individuals' enlightened self-interest was.[47] Rather than labor, frugality and industriousness being seen as necessary means to wealth, or as moral qualities that one class enjoyed and others lacked, Say's political economy implied that these virtues were indispensable to republicanism, and certainly not the exclusive property of one particular class. The goal of Say's political economy was not luxurious wealth for the few, but comfort for all:

> commerce would create a nation whose people lived 'in ease rather than in opulence, where everyone knew how to read...where there are no unproductive individuals who are a burden on society, and no poor men who cannot, with labour and good conduct, win an easy subsistence, and lead the kind of life which the English call *comfortable*.'[48]

Even Say's *Traité d'économie politique*, first published in 1803, so often seen as the means by which Say popularized the *laissez-faire* Adam Smith, identified two key goals of political economy. The first was to point out that *all* citizens contributed to the wealth of society, that all citizens were industrious, and that the republican, commercial state required the efforts of all. The second goal was to offer the means of eliminating poverty.[49] Say's lack of fit with either the second generation of orthodox "liberal" political economists in

France, or with the classical political economists of Great Britain, can be seen, then, in his commitment to eradicating poverty (and thus to the solution of "social questions")[50]; his lack of dogmatism about state intervention[51]; his commitment to inculcating republican manners; and his belief that his political economy only made sense—and only worked—within a new society characterized by "enlightened self-interest," a term which itself meant something very different than orthodox economists believed.[52]

If the Adam Smith and Jean-Baptiste Say who many nineteenth-century French economists felt they knew so well were indeed historical myths, then when and why were these myths created? Historians have pointed to the radical changes that took place in the years between the death of Adam Smith in 1790 and the death of Say in 1832 as explanation for why Say and Smith came to be understood so very differently by their successors than by their contemporaries.[53] According to Emma Rothschild, the familiar partnership between *laissez-faire* economics and political conservatism occurred after the French Revolution and the Napoleonic Wars.[54] The perceived excesses of the French Revolution, and particularly the violence and radicalism of the Terror, decoupled the new science of political economy from the movement of reform, and re-coupled it to the movement of conservatism; as Rothschild writes: "in a conflict between gradual change and Revolutionary violence, the liberals were on the side of the slow and the consensual; in a conflict between freedom of individual property and violent expropriation, they were on the side of property."[55] Also decoupled were economic reform and political reform (Rothschild describes this process as reconstructing political economy as "an innocuous, unpolitical subject"[56]), with the result that political economy could now be portrayed as a technical science, politically innocuous and unconcerned with political commentary and political reform, and Adam Smith and Jean-Baptiste Say as "retiring, innocuous sorts of persons," rather than Enlightenment *philosophes*.[57] In short, the hopeful conditions under which both Adam Smith and Jean-Baptiste Say wrote had begun to change by 1815, shifting the natural allies of those espousing *laissez-faire* economics, and changing the context in which Smith and Say's ideas could be read and the meanings that could be attributed to their ideas.[58] As political liberals gained power, they claimed Adam Smith and Jean-Baptiste Say as their own. With the accession of the constitutional monarch Louis-Philippe, liberalism had been established in France, and was seeking to establish an historical tradition for itself. Thus, its adherents looked backward in time and claimed predecessors, ancestors, forefathers: men like Voltaire, Montesquieu, and Turgot, but also

Adam Smith and Jean-Baptiste Say.[59] As the strength and power of manufacture grew, industrialists found within the work of Smith and Say a justification for their activities, a validation for their material wealth, and "scientific" support for the principles of *laissez faire* and government non-intervention.

By the 1830s in France, then, the science of political economy was understood by its practitioners in ways that its founders may not have fully recognized. For French political economists in the 1830s, political economy was a narrowly-defined, inflexible science that rested upon a handful of universal laws, unchanging and unchangeable, true for all times and all places. The most fundamental of those laws was that which maintained the existence of a balanced, harmonious, self-regulating market, and which thus dictated a *laissez-faire* attitude with regard to all government activities. For economic historian Edgar Allix, writing in 1911 about early nineteenth-century political economy, it was Charles Dunoyer who more than any other French economist of the period embodied this new post-Smith, post-Say "scientific" political economy. According to Allix, however, Dunoyer's was an unfortunate and detrimental re-reading of political economy:

> As for Dunoyer, he narrowed the liberal doctrine into a doctrine of bourgeois resistance against the popular class, and he turned the point of all economic arguments against workers. With him, liberalism lost its scientific serenity and illustrated the truth that a doctrine which forms under opposition, deforms in power.[60]

Of course, French economists writing after Jean-Baptiste Say and alongside Charles Dunoyer had not yet come to Allix's conclusion. While Dunoyer's ideas were extreme even among his economist colleagues, it was nonetheless this scientific framework within which early nineteenth-century French economists operated: the self-regulating mechanism of the market economy, the natural harmony of interests, the inviolable right of individual self-determination, and *laissez-faire*. This, then, was the political economy inherited and practiced by the economists of the first half of the century in France, the political economy whose practitioners were desperate to see granted institutional status and authority. But it was also this political economy—elegant, simple, scientific, uncluttered by real-life details, certain in its adherence to the principle of *laissez-faire*—that would come under question by the mid-nineteenth century because of those messy real-life details that did not quite fit into the stream-lined science that political economy had become.

The Practitioners and Profession of French Political Economy

Who were the men who answered to the label of "political economist" in the first half of the nineteenth century in France, the men who inherited from Adam Smith and Jean-Baptiste Say what they understood to be an objective and concrete science, akin to physics in its use of observation, deduction, and logic?[61] By profession they were a diverse group: doctors, lawyers, engineers, surveyors, industrialists, and politicians. Most of these men came to political economy through something else, whether another profession, a personal relationship, or a political event. Charles Dunoyer and Louis Wolowski were first trained in the law. A surveyor, Théodore Fix came to political economy through his translations of a work of German political economy into French, and in 1833 founded a journal, the *Revue mensuelle d'économie politique.* Originally from Marseille, Louis Reybaud had been both a sailor and merchant until his arrival in Paris in 1828. Louis-René Villermé, best known for his work in public hygiene but a close compatriot of French political economists in the first half of the century, was trained as a doctor. Jerome-Adolphe Blanqui, who had first studied medicine and chemistry, became a friend and protégé of Jean-Baptiste Say, who introduced the young Blanqui to the "classic" works of political economy. Joseph Garnier was himself a student and friend of Blanqui's, and attended Blanqui's courses at the *École supérieure de commerce.* Gilbert-Urbain Guillaumin, who founded the *Librairie Guillaumin* which published most of the key works on political economy in France during the nineteenth century, including the *Journal des économistes,* became devoted to the science and cause of political economy after attending Blanqui's course on *économie industrielle* at the *Conservatoire des arts et métiers* in the 1830s. Most of these men were supporters of the July Revolution in 1830, and found political economy, as it was then understood in France, to be a natural ally of the new political regime, although a few professed more deeply-rooted republican sentiments.[62] For others, it was the events of 1848, rather than 1830, that seem to have sparked their interest in political economy.[63]

Given that political economy was a new science, without a professionalized system of training, most of these men were autodidacts, even as they spent years writing and publishing in the field. For most of them, professional development consisted of teaching themselves through consultation with the key works of political economy, or of forming personal acquaintances with economists of standing (Jean-Baptiste Say, for instance) and acquiring the training that came from (one imagines) regular discussions with them. A few of them had perhaps attended one of the few courses taught by political economists in France in the early part of the century, Say's course at the *Conservatoire des arts et métiers*, for instance, or Blanqui's at the *École supérieure de commerce*.[64]

Only for a very few men was their training in political economy a source of income: Jerome-Adolphe Blanqui, for instance, who was the director of the *École supérieure de commerce* from 1830 until 1854, and held the chair of *économie industrielle* at the *Conservatoire des arts et métiers* from 1833 until his death in 1854; or Michel Chevalier, who held the chair of political economy at the *Collège de France* from 1840 to 1850; or Joseph Garnier, who held the chair of political economy at the *École des Ponts et Chaussées* from 1846 to 1881. But these were individual chairs, not departments; there were only a handful of such posts, and while they were often handed down from one member of the political economic community to another, it meant that only a handful of political economists could teach political economy from a lectern at any given time.

For even fewer were their writings a source of income. There is no evidence to suggest that publication of articles in the *Journal des économistes* earned contributors an income (and all of the men associated with the discipline of political economy in the nineteenth century were regular contributors to the *Journal*). Many of these men wrote and published quite copiously, whether articles or full economic tomes; some enjoyed money prizes by winning competitions sponsored by the *Académie des sciences morales et politiques*.[65] But for most of these men, even those who won prizes and published regularly, it is likely that family money, a separate career (even if eventually abandoned), or an alternate source of income (from a government post, for instance), provided them with the opportunity to write, read, publish, and speak on political economy. A description of economist Louis Wolowski in a recent book on the *Conservatoire des arts et métiers* referred to him as "jurist, historian, economist, publicist, politician, member of several academies, and professor," a title that seems to suggest not only the professional biographies of many of these men, but something of their financial means.[66]

Many of these men seem to have aspired to political careers, some of them enjoying quite successful ones. Under the July Monarchy, for instance, Charles Dunoyer was the Prefect of the department of the Allier, then of the Somme. In 1846 Louis Reybaud, Jerome-Adolphe Blanqui, and Léon

Faucher won seats in the Chamber of Deputies, Reybaud from Marseilles, Blanqui from the Gironde, and Faucher from Reims.[67] Frédéric Bastiat was elected as a deputy from Bordeaux to the Constitutional Assembly in 1848. Jean-Gustave Courcelle-Seneuil had a political career under the Third Republic, as did Joseph Garnier, who was elected senator from the Alpes-Maritimes in 1876.

Aside from their interest in, or devotion to, the science of political economy, what united these men were the institutions that economist Charles Gide, late in the nineteenth century, would describe as strongholds of the profession of French political economy.[68] The *Conservatoire des arts et métiers* and its chair of *économie industrielle*; the *Collège de France* and its chair of *économie politique*; the *Académie des sciences morales et politiques*, to which most French political economists were elected; the *Journal des économistes* and the *Société d'économie politique*: all these institutions brought French political economists together in a common effort to advance their science, and to lobby the French state on behalf of their jurisdictional claims.

Particularly during the Restoration, however, the science of political economy existed in an awkward and sometimes hostile relationship with the bureaucratic French state, a particular problem for the new discipline given its need to see its jurisdictional claims recognized and rewarded by academic posts. Under the Restoration government, political economy was considered both religiously and politically subversive. Insofar as political economists were considered to be "liberals," a title that most economists themselves embraced, the new science was deemed at odds with the politics of the *Ultras*. Many economists were opposed—some quite vociferously—to the Bourbons and their policies, hardly a stance guaranteed to assure governmental approbation and thus professional favors.[69] While it is true it was under the Restoration that Say published the third and fourth editions of his *Traité d'économie politique*, that the first chair of political economy in France was established in 1819 at the *Faculté de Droit de Paris*, and that Say was granted the chair of *économie industrielle* at the *Conservatoire des arts et métiers*, it is also true that no one was ever named to that chair at the *Faculté de Droit*, effectively abolishing it, and that Say's course in *économie industrielle* was confined to the *Conservatoire*, "far from all the great establishments of public instruction, as if someone were fearful that it might be attended by young people destined for the liberal professions."[70] Economists' support of the July Revolution, and of the July Monarchy in general, meant that relations with the state improved after 1830, a shift evidenced by the establishment of new academic posts. But even under the July Monarchy, economists' dogmatic opposition to protectionist policies earned them enemies within government circles.[71]

This rocky relationship between political economists and the French state meant that economists' desire to see their jurisdictional claims recognized and compensated by academic posts and professional status would be neither easily nor quickly satisfied. French political economists would have to become a proactive group, energetically promoting their science. After the July Revolution in 1830 their goal was threefold: to disprove the supposed political subversiveness of the discipline; to give it a scientific legitimacy and thus rescue it from the isolation of technical education; and to publicize the basic tenets of the science.[72]

Aside from the unfilled chair of political economy at the *Faculté de Droit de Paris*, it was the *Conservatoire des arts et métiers* that in 1820 established the first permanent chair of economic science in France. The *Conservatoire* had been transformed under the Restoration from a museum housing items related to industry—tools, machines, inventions—into a technical institute whose goal was the "application of scientific knowledge to commerce and industry."[73] As a private, technical school, the *Conservatoire* operated far from the traditional and well-established Faculties of Letters, Law, Sciences, Medicine, and Pharmacy.[74] It offered courses that were open to the public, and free, with the goal of spreading the latest scientific knowledge and demonstrating its application to the practical realm.[75] Like another unique French institution, the *Collège de France*, there were no regular students at the *Conservatoire*, but rather auditors. Attending classes was purely voluntary, and did not lead to a degree; no controls were placed upon registration or attendance.[76] Much of the *Conservatoire*'s "student body" consisted of workers, artisans, and small employers, although Say's courses in political economy tended to attract a more specialized audience.[77] And if Say's courses were "a bit austere," his successor Adolphe Blanqui's were very popular, with working-class attendees outnumbering all other members of the regular audiences.[78]

When the chair of economic science was created at the *Conservatoire*, its first title-holder, Jean-Baptiste Say, was not named to a chair of *économie politique*, but rather to a chair of *économie industrielle*. Administrators at the *Conservatoire* believed that the name *économie industrielle* would allay concerns that an economic science course would discuss public and political issues, off-limits during the Restoration. In keeping with this attempt to distance the school from the supposedly suspicious nature of political economy, Say drew a distinction between political and industrial economy. In his opening lecture in December of 1820, Say pointed out that:

> When one says political economy, one means nothing other than the knowledge of laws that preside over the wealth of a society, and over the persons who together constitute that society. When one says industrial economy, one means the understanding of laws that preside over wealth for the use of people who are involved in the industrial professions.[79]

Whether or not Say succeeded in drawing this distinction (and economist Joseph Garnier argued later in the century that the distinction, already a fine one in theory, did not hold in practice[80]), he clearly tried to describe—or felt as if he needed to describe—his course in *économie industrielle* as a practical business course rather than a theoretical economics one.

Upon Say's death in 1832, his seat was assumed by Jerome-Adolphe Blanqui, who also continued to hold the directorship of the *École supérieure de commerce*, to which he had been appointed in 1830. It had been at the private *École supérieure de commerce de Paris* that political economy was first integrated as part of a degree program that trained men entering the world of commerce. In 1824, Jean-Baptiste Say had led the successful effort to establish a chair in *histoire et l'économie industrielle* at the *École*, a post granted in 1825 to Adolphe Blanqui and held by him until his death in 1854.[81]

In 1831 French political economy enjoyed another stroke of luck when the government created a chair of *économie politique* at the *Collège de France*. The post was awarded to Say, who held it until his death a year later. His successor, hand-picked by Prime Minister François Guizot himself, was Pellegrino Rossi, who taught at the *Collège* until he was replaced by the young *Polytechnicien* Michel Chevalier in 1840. Like the *Conservatoire*, the *Collège de France* had no official students, and courses led to no professional degree. Rather, the primary function of the *Collège de France* was to offer a site for the teaching of subjects that had not been accepted elsewhere, "free from all constraints of certification and open to disinterested research."[82] Despite the varied audiences at the two institutions—courses at the *Collège* attracted an audience from a decidedly more privileged social class than courses at the *Conservatoire*—both the chairs of political economy at the *Collège de France* and of industrial economy at the *Conservatoire des arts et métiers* would be important sites from which nineteenth-century French economists attempted to publicize their science, gain recognition, and stake a professional claim to the scientific study of the economy.

Alongside the *Collège de France* and the *Conservatoire des arts et métiers* were the other indispensable sites of nineteenth-century political economy's self-promotion: the *Académie des sciences morales et politiques,* a national "think-tank," and in particular, its *section d'économie politique*; and the *Journal des économistes* and its accompanying social club, the *Société d'économie politique.* Founded in 1795, suppressed in 1803 by Napoleon, and re-founded in 1832 by François Guizot, the *Académie* convened intellectuals of various disciplines, ideological commitments, and political inclinations.[83] The essay competitions sponsored by the *Académie* offered political economists a means of publicizing both the basic tenets of their science and their scientific opinions on particular economic matters. Equally importantly, the competitions, and their money prizes, offered financial support to men largely without professional posts.[84] The list of economists elected to the *Académie* during the nineteenth century reads as a "who's who" of French political economy: Jerome-Adolphe Blanqui, Louis Reybaud, Louis-René Villermé, Henri Baudrillart, Joseph Garnier, Louis Wolowski, Émile Levasseur.

Most of the economists associated with the *Académie des sciences morales et politiques* enjoyed both the public and private forums provided by the publisher Gilbert-Urbain Guillaumin, who has been described as one of those "unknowns who makes history."[85] Inspired by Blanqui's teaching at the *Conservatoire des arts et métiers* in the early 1830s, Guillaumin opened a bookstore devoted to the subject of political economy. The next step, in January 1835, was to open a publishing house, *Guillaumin et Compagnie,* supported by wealthy French liberals as well as merchants, men who shared a commitment to free trade and anti-protectionism, and who thus supported—both financially and ideologically—the claims of political economists. By the 1840s, the catalog of *Guillaumin et Compagnie* included the work of the French Physiocrats, Adam Smith, Jean-Baptiste Say, Jerome-Adolphe Blanqui, Louis Reybaud, Thomas Malthus, David Ricardo, Simonde de Sismondi, and Pellegrino Rossi.

Another brainchild of Guillaumin was the *Société des Économistes.* The *Société* was formed in November 1842 with five members: Guillaumin himself, Joseph Garnier, Adolphe Blaise, Eugène Daire, and Pierre Bos, who soon left the political economy camp for the protectionists (and was therefore derisively left unnamed by the brief history of the *Société* in the *Annales de la Société d'économie politique*).[86] The *Société* was, if not a formal professional organization (since political economy was not a formal academic profession), at least an informal one that united most practitioners, whether professional or amateur, and that lobbied on behalf of political economy to the government. By 1847, having changed its name to the *Société d'Économie Politique*, membership had reached fifty members.[87] The *Société* operated in a visibly different mode than the *Académie des sciences morales et politiques*; instead of an exclusively academic forum, Guillaumin organized the *Société* as a club that gathered monthly for dinner and casual conversation about economic matters.[88]

But of all of Guillaumin's contributions to the history of French political economy, it was his publication of the *Journal des économistes* that quite possibly mattered the most. Throughout the nineteenth century, the *Journal des économistes* was the principal organ of French political economy, its publishing history spanning four successive governments, from the July Monarchy to the end of the Third Republic.[89] Published for the first time in December of 1841, the *Journal* was conceived by political economists not only as an academic journal, but also as a means of publicity for their new science.[90] It was used as a place of theoretical musings, a place for sharing economic ideas and their applications, a place of community. It was also a site from which economists could publicly voice their jurisdictional claims on behalf of political economy, a crucial site, in other words, of self-promotion.

Writers and editors for the *Journal* included all of the men who understood themselves to be the inheritors of the science founded by Adam Smith and Jean-Baptiste Say. The format of the *Journal* in these first twenty-five years changed little.[91] Each issue contained six or seven articles touching on a variety of subjects concerning political economy, book reviews of national and international publications, notes of the meetings, discussions, and debates of the *Société d'Économie Politique*, and various short notices concerning new, proposed, or defeated economic and social legislation. Instead of a purely theoretical, academic journal, the *Journal des économistes* set out to offer examinations of practical, concrete situations, and to apply scientific theory—the core of which economists presumed—to these actual circumstances.[92] The audience for the *Journal*, then, was a general audience: an educated audience, to be sure, but nonetheless a public, non-academic, non-professional audience.

The other crucial audience for the *Journal des économistes* was quite evidently the French state, which controlled educational posts and thus by extension political economy's reputation and status as a science. As practitioners of an aspiring academic discipline with only a few institutional anchors, it was to the state—through general public opinion—that economists addressed their jurisdictional claims over the propagation of economic truths, truths that represented socially-useful knowledge that to date had been repressed or constrained, with the result that society was neither as productive nor as healthy as it could be. The work of political economy, according to an 1818 letter from Jean-Baptiste Say to the Baron Thénard of the *Académie des sciences,* was to destroy the erroneous ideas about the economy held by so many people whose interests were tied up with it. The work of political economy was not simply to uncover, analyze, and understand natural economic laws, but to make them known:

> How many false ideas, how many false notions about the true nature of those things which concern them, can be found widespread among the class of merchants and manufacturers! Whose conversations so often indicate so little education! They hardly know the value of the words they use; they attribute commercial incidents to causes which play absolutely no part; they anticipate results which are outside the realm of the possible....It is thus necessary in France to destroy many of the prejudices which prevent us from properly deciding upon questions which stem from industry; it is necessary to spread many of the notions which are already common knowledge elsewhere...[93]

It was political economists who understood how the economy worked, who understood the laws that governed the production, consumption, and distribution of wealth, and who could therefore publicize their understanding, for the good of all. In short, as Louis Reybaud argued in 1841, political economy "was at the heart of all questions being discussed and all problems that trouble."[94]

As specialists in a science of observation which lay "at the heart of all questions," French economists also considered themselves to be experts whose opinions, theories, and advice ought to guide government policy.[95] The French state's economic policies were erratic, economist Hippolyte Dussard argued in 1843:

> adopting no absolute principle, proceeding according to the needs of the day, leaning to the left, then to the right, then finally regaining an equilibrium, like a drunken man, rather than marching straight along a path like a cool-headed man; conceding to one, then to another; making up for today's mistake with tomorrow's mistake; wanting to please everyone and ending up by discontenting the nation; this is the current art of men of state who aim for practicability....On the contrary, principles ought to be the

> basis of every measure, of every act emanating from authority...if principles are not a beacon that guides, there will never be anything stable, nothing firm, nothing fixed...[96]

It was this belief that political economy had something—or rather, everything—to contribute to the health and welfare of the French nation that lay at the heart of economists' demands for more academic posts. Political economy ought to be taught not only to the upper classes, one economist argued in 1845, but to industrialists, the middle class, even workers.[97] The results of the dissemination and promulgation of political economic tenets would be far-reaching and socially-beneficial: the young manufacturer could now learn, not through trial-and-error, but through science; workers would come to understand the importance of thrift, savings, and foresight, and to recognize the possibility of self-improvement; and the French state would no longer have to battle unenlightened public opinion in its efforts to implement wise economic policies.[98]

A Promising Science?

In 1840, the future of French political economy appeared auspicious. By that year, political economy had benefited from the support of a relatively sympathetic government, and economists had every reason to believe that support would grow. Political economists held several important academic posts and believed that active self-promotion by their discipline's organizational structures would result in more. Inspired by the presumed significance of their science, its history, and their predecessors, economists were unwavering in their efforts to gain professional status for themselves and their science. Anchoring that science were particular tenets, to which most economists were committed and whose veracity was assured by their status as "natural laws." The *Journal des économistes* offered French economists a place from which to publicize the basic tenets of their science to both public opinion and the French state for the good of society as a whole. Finally, evidence of industrial transformation in France appeared to be proving the truth of economists' scientific tenets. By the 1830s, France's industrial development had proceeded to such a degree that political economists were able not simply to theorize about it, but to judge, assess, and compare it. But while in 1840 French economists believed that the institutional and political outlook for political economy was hopeful, what was nonetheless worrying was the evidence from the world outside Paris and the confines of the *Collège de*

France, the *Conservatoire des arts et métiers* and the *Académie des sciences morales et politiques.* Despite believing themselves to be practicing a science and confidently looking forward to that science's further advancement, what disturbed political economists was awkward information "from the field," information that suggested that France's industrial transformation was having unexpected and harmful effects, particularly among those workers employed in newly-mechanizing industries.

Significantly, one of the institutions disseminating this awkward information was the *Académie des sciences morales et politiques*, whose members commissioned a study of working-class conditions by public hygienist Louis-René Villermé. Based upon data gathered between 1835 and 1837, and published in 1840, Villermé's *Tableau de l'état physique et moral des ouvriers employés dans les manufactures de cotton, de laine et de soie* offered a gloomy picture of conditions among workers employed in France's textile industries. Whatever Villermé's "keen enthusiasm for the vast productive potential of mechanization,"[99] and whatever the ambiguity of his explanations for working-class misery, there was no doubt that the portrait of working-class lives in the *Tableau* was far from rosy. And while the backing provided by the *Académie des sciences morales et politiques* lent credence to Villermé's claims, it also meant that this gloomy picture was widely circulated and widely known. For political economists, this publicity for awkward and worrisome data could only have been unwelcome.

The gloomy picture of the consequences of industrialization provoked vocal criticism from a variety of directions. From social Catholics came a critique of the moral decline that had resulted from the industrialization process.[100] Evidence of miserable workers, unearthed by Villermé's *Tableau*, only served to reinforce the argument that working-class misery was due to a spiritual decline brought about by factory labor, immoral working and living conditions, and the decay of the patriarchal family. For social Catholics, the solution was neither to rely upon individuals' inherent capacity for reason and appropriate self-determination, nor to accept misery as the only incentive to good behavior and rational decisions, but rather to reestablish the moral community that was once French society: to strengthen the family, to uphold Catholicism, and to convince superiors of their moral obligation and responsibility to their inferiors, and inferiors of their allegiance to their superiors. French socialists aired a different, but no less worrying, critique. For utopian socialists, the true nature of capitalism and the society that accompanied it would never accommodate the natural inclinations of human beings. Human beings were creative, emotional, and capricious; the discipline, monotony, and diligence required by industrial capitalism meant that human beings had to undergo a fundamental change in order to conform to the new capitalist society. Human misery was thus caused not only by the disorganization of capitalism, but by this poor fit between capitalism and human nature. According to socialists, solutions to human misery lay in the reorganization of the economy and the labor process in accordance with real human nature.

Even more unsettling for French economists must have been the realization that many of their colleagues–if not, most disconcertingly, they themselves–had begun to display a surprising repugnance for the most egregious effects of "liberty" and industry in France. Despite all the presumably scientific justifications of working-class misery and of a *laissez-faire* approach toward that misery, by the time both industry and misery were present in France in noticeable quantities, many economists found themselves discomfited by the prospect of sitting by and watching while workers lived short, nasty, and brutish lives as they (supposedly) learned to become more rational, moral, and thrifty.[101] In 1841, then, the appearance of the first volume of the *Journal des économistes*, the product of twenty years of hard work and self-promotion, was cause for much celebration among French political economists. But, more ominously, that first volume would also reveal the doubts plaguing the science of political economy and its advocates, and would foreshadow the disciplinary dilemmas that economists would have to confront during the rest of the century.

2. Political Economy and *la question sociale*

In his introductory essay to the first volume of the *Journal des économistes*, published in 1841, political economist Louis Reybaud made a remarkable confession. Political economy, he admitted, the science that had once enjoyed a common language and common assumptions, had now succumbed to a confusion of opinions and ideas, continuous assaults upon its authority, "an invasion of more and more detestable jargon," and the appearance of "as many systems as heads."[1] As a result, Reybaud argued, political economists were suffering a crisis of confidence in their own science. "The only remedy for this situation," he argued, "would be in a sincere return to the principles that the masters of the science proclaimed, and the cessation of this indiscipline which seems to make of our economists a corps of partisans and not a regular army."[2]

Behind Reybaud's conservative solution, however, lay a more radical admission. Political economy, Reybaud divulged, had so far been unable to solve the collective problems of the French working class, commonly known as *la question sociale*, or "the social question." Although Reybaud did not use the term *la question sociale* in his essay, referring instead to "social difficulties," the "accidents of industrial life," and "diverse industrial and commercial infirmities," he nonetheless elaborated a host of social problems that were regularly grouped as *la question sociale* during the nineteenth century: the hunger suffered by people who had been replaced by machines; the illnesses suffered by the working young and old; the coalitions of workers against masters, and the monopolies of masters against workers. While Reybaud maintained that an inability to find solutions to pressing issues was a situation faced by all sciences, he nonetheless implied that political economy's particular failure marked a crossroads for his science.[3] The masters of the science had solved the questions of value, capital, supply and demand, wages, taxes, and monopolies, but what remained was what Reybaud called the "living part" of the science, what he suggested was the use of economic science to improve the condition of all producers, whether of the owning or the laboring classes.[4] If political economy had been accused of paying more attention to objects than to men, economists needed to confront this charge.[5] There was no greater reason for studying political economy, Reybaud noted, than to assist in the solution of the problems of labor, and economists needed to be willing, he implied, to admit the failures of their analyses thus far:

> Like all human knowledge, political economy has its doubts, its miscalculations, its chasms. It understands that the wealth of a people rests in its labor, but it has yet to find the law of distributive justice by which quantity of labor can determine that of enjoyment. It is unaware of the means by which to spare those unhappy people displaced by machines and left unemployed by competition from the tortures of hunger. Without the help of morality and charity, it can do nothing either for children weakened while still young, or for the elderly whose strength is consumed by industry. The natural equilibrium which political economy proclaims and which it invokes does not suffice therefore for calming all the agonies and for supporting all existences.[6]

Why was Reybaud's a remarkable confession? For many of his predecessors and contemporaries, political economy was a natural science not unlike the exact sciences of physics, mathematics, and chemistry. Whether or not Reybaud and his colleagues had misread or misunderstood Jean-Baptiste Say's writings on political economy, they had always understood the science to which Say had contributed to be an abstract, universal, and theoretical one. Say had written of the need to apply the experimental methods of the physical sciences to political economy, treating social events as analogous to the physical reactions studied by chemists and physicists. Like physics, he argued, political economy was an objective and concrete science that could be studied by observation, deduction, and logic. It was the misfortune of Say's successors, however, to have discerned the significant differences between the science of physics and that of political economy. By the time Reybaud offered his confessions, political economists had recognized that they faced problems shared by few physical scientists: the difficulty of observation; the impossibility of experimentation; the inadequacy of scientific dispassion when dealing with human lives; the nagging ethical sentiment that asserted that working-class poverty would never be socially and morally desirable no matter how warranted it might appear to be; and the uncomfortable realization that behind the abstract, universal, and scientific category of Labor lay real flesh-and-blood human beings who might need direction, correction, regulation, and management, in short, government, evocatively defined by sociologist Giovanna Procacci as "a form of activity aimed at shaping other people's conduct."[7] Reybaud's essay is not—at least in its ordinary meaning—historically significant. It is, however, one of those seemingly minor and largely forgotten texts so useful for their ability to access moments of uncertainty, rupture, or discontinuity, and to suggest issues of broader social significance. The importance of Reybaud's essay lies in the spotlight that it shines on the dilemma that *la question sociale* represented for political economy precisely at the moment of economists' greatest confidence in the scientific nature of their discipline.

This chapter investigates the relationship between *la question sociale* and the embryonic discipline that was French political economy from, roughly, 1830 to 1850, the period when the social question emerged on the public stage as the key target of social apprehension, and the first attempts at its solution appeared. In the first part of this chapter I turn to French industrialists, the most prolific observers of *la question sociale,* to describe the problems and anxieties that comprised this social question, and to examine their preferred solution, industrial paternalism. I then turn to the work of Michel Foucault to explore in greater depth the problem of discipline that underlay industrialists' understanding and portrayal of *la question sociale* and the paternalist solution. Following Foucault, I argue that paternalism was a creative, rather than repressive, system of power; that paternalist projects were designed to alleviate social misery by creating disciplined bodies out of undisciplined and thus miserable workers, and by creating workers capable of disciplining themselves. In the third part of this chapter, I analyze the challenge that *la question sociale* and industrialists' paternalist solution posed for the discipline of political economy. If left unchecked, *la question sociale* appeared to threaten French political stability and economic development, hence political economists' advocacy of the industrial paternalist solution. On the other hand, how were political economists to include "government"—something that theoretically ought not to be a part of it—into the economic science, resting as it did upon the universal law of *laissez-faire*? *La question sociale,* and political economists' growing support of its paternalist solution, thus appeared to disprove economists' own theories, which in turn threatened to simultaneously undermine the claims of political economy to institutional status on the grounds of scientific authority, and to open the way for state intervention into on-going industrial development.

La question sociale and its Paternalist Solution

The "social difficulties" that Louis Reybaud's essay exposed constitute what contemporaries and historians alike have labeled *la question sociale*, a broad category encompassing working-class misery, growing antagonism between workers and employers, the appearance and spread of socialist doctrines, and working-class indiscipline. *La question sociale* represented, then, all the unexpected effects of, and responses to, industrial capitalism.[8] It was the recognition that industrialization had had brutal social consequences, the worst excesses of which might need to be mitigated.

La question sociale had not only economic causes and implications, but political ones as well. It was not simply an unexpected result of French industrial development in the early nineteenth century, but also a consequence of the political turmoil inherited from the French Revolution, of the difficult process of remaking both a new society and its citizens. It was, as sociologist Giovanna Procacci has noted, not only a discursive space for the discussion, for instance, of whether building individual homes for workers would relieve daily misery, but also a space for the discussion of what misery meant for French society, and how miserable and visibly unequal citizens were to be invited into a society founded upon fraternity and equality.[9] *La question sociale*, or the problem of misery and all its causes and consequences, was thus a threat not just to individual workers suffering from unemployment, malnutrition, and ill health, but to a society rethinking the nature of the responsibilities between citizens and the state.[10]

It was the broad nature of the threat that lent discussions of *la question sociale* their sense of urgency, and that explains the wide variety of contributors to those discussions. No single group (even political economists, who became vocal contributors to debates over *la question sociale)* ever dominated the public conversation about *la question sociale*, nor did contributors ever fully agree either on its causes, its consequences, or its solutions. *La question sociale* was, then, a broad and malleable category that could incorporate a wide variety of contemporary social problems, and invite a diverse array of participants, perspectives, and solutions.

Although no one dominated conversations about *la question sociale*, French industrialists were without a doubt among the first and most influential publicists of *la question sociale*. It was French industrialists who pointed out the unexpected results of industrialization, and who thus drew attention to the social problems that political economists would experience as a threat to the coherence and self-confidence of their science. It was also French industrialists who proposed and championed the paternalist solution to *la question sociale* that economists would study, promote, and graft onto their science. The descriptions of *la question sociale* that follow, then, are drawn from French industrialists, who most immediately and personally felt the political and economic threat that working-class misery posed.

Among their workers French industrialists noted problems that ranged from the most obvious issues of wages, working conditions, and discipline, to political matters—for instance, the question of the working-class vote and the spread of socialist ideas—to more personal and private questions of individual behavior and morality. *La question sociale* thus entailed the problems of overworked and undisciplined workers; underfed and neglected children; abused wives; crowded and unsanitary homes; alcoholism and promiscuity; strikes and riots; and workers' supposed susceptibility to what industrialists understood as revolutionary political doctrines. Central, however, to this diverse array of problems that formed *la question sociale* was the complaint, sometimes expressed explicitly, other times left implicit, that French workers suffered from a lack of discipline, both private and public, both on the job and at home. And thus, industrialists implied, because workers were unable to discipline themselves, because they were unable to control, regulate, or correct themselves, they could not be left alone.

Industrialists regularly bemoaned what they saw as being a lack of efficiency, discipline and loyalty among their workers. In an 1849 report written by a Saône-et-Loire departmental commission, the authors pointed to the connection between "moral" workers and disciplined workers:

> Without moralization, in fact, one cannot obtain from a considerable mass of workers the discipline, order, regularity of labor, and even the devotion which are necessary for an active production.[11]

Factory regulations, or *règlements d'atelier*, which firms began to post in workshops during the early years of the nineteenth century, give a sense of what manufacturers saw to be workers' habitual behavior and activities, and how this workplace behavior worried them.[12] These regulations typically mentioned unexplained absences, insubordination, lack of respect or disobedience, obscene graffiti on factory property, refusal to execute tasks, negative attitudes or negligence in the execution of tasks, abandonment of posts, insults or threats between workers, insults or threats to factory personnel or visitors, drunkenness, consumption of alcohol at work, theft, use of factory material or machinery to make objects designed for workers' personal use, and actions designed to impede productivity.

If the inefficient execution of their work disturbed the pace of production and raised labor costs, workers' apparent unwillingness to follow orders also seemed to exemplify the general indifference they felt toward their employers' interests. In a report to the Industrial Society of Mulhouse, one Dr. Weber noted:

> On his part, the workers feels no sense of attachment to his master....He does not identify himself with his master in order to contribute to the success of the establishment, he does not see his master's prosperity as being in his own self-interest. Instead, he treats his master as an enemy who exploits him, he cheats him consciously, or at least, he does not look after the interests of his master as if they were his own, and lets his master go about his business with perfect indifference.[13]

While the mistrustful relationship between workers and employers was thought to compromise the productivity and profitability of French industry, it also endangered the health of society more generally. Manufacturers' fears of workers' economic and social shortcomings often gave rise to suspicions about their potential for violent and revolutionary political disorder. The July Revolution of 1830, the Lyonnais uprisings of 1831 and 1832, the 1848 Revolution, as well as the popularity of socialist ideas among certain segments of the working class, seemed to give credence to manufacturers' suspicions that the working class was capable of violent agitation.[14] The Lyonnais uprising, for instance, was documented with precision by the departmental officials and manufacturers in Alsace. In fact, throughout the nineteenth century, departmental officials sought to record workers' collective mood, to investigate all rumors of rebellion in the manufacturing city of Mulhouse, and to establish plans to suppress any social disorders that might occur.[15] Concern for social order seems also to have been at the root of manufacturers' interest in providing workers with an education. In 1853, industrialist M. Hartmann Leibach described how a moral education based on evangelical principles could diminish antagonism and discontent between classes: "I say it with deep conviction: sufficient moral education and instruction, this is the basis of public order, of prosperity and of security for all."[16]

But if *la question sociale* often took the form of complaints about workers not working properly, not exhibiting the proper degree of loyalty and commitment to their employers, and even working, however unwittingly, *against* their employers, it also entailed recognition of the decline in workers' material conditions and the misery in which many French workers lived. Participants in discussions of *la question sociale* seldom agreed upon their explanations for this misery and their proposed solutions for its alleviation. But most did seem to agree that too many French workers were living short, hungry, unhealthy, and unhappy lives. "How precarious is their existence," the editors of the *Bulletin de la Société Industrielle de Mulhouse* wrote in 1828:

> when one thinks of the vicissitudes to which the working class is particularly subject. If industry or commerce experience a crisis, or if sicknesses and the infirmities of old age, ordinary companions of life, afflict the worker, he falls immediately to the charge of the public commiseration; this is often the fate, not just of the single worker, but of an entire family.[17]

The apparent absence of working-class family life struck and horrified many observers. Working-class parents—and most notably the father—were often depicted as weak and ignorant, and thus incapable of providing their children with the proper education and moral values. Contemporaries noted that many workers married early in life, before they had the financial resources to support a family, and then ended up abandoning their wives and children. Alsatian industrialist Daniel Le Grand described how the abdication of parental responsibility and corrosion of paternal authority had reversed the "natural" order of things in working-class families:

> These young boys of 6 to 12 years of age, already with pipes in their mouths, oaths and obscene proposals on their lips, brandy as their beverage and dust as their seasoning, becoming fathers when they ought to still be school children, propagating large families by the most shameful and pernicious of speculations so as to even more quickly abandon themselves to laziness and drunkenness with their companions, who are equally depraved; to be fed by their children at an age when they should be feeding them themselves, and thus reversing all the bases of paternal authority.[18]

According to many manufacturers, then, working-class family life had either ceased to exist or had become perverted, the normal affection between children and their parents replaced by indifference, or in the worst cases, by the exploitation or abandonment of children by their parents.[19]

Many participants in discussions of *la question sociale* voiced specific concerns about the effects of industrial work on women and on the structure of the family, arguing that female wage labor threatened the moral and physical health of the household.[20] But as they were often portrayed, women were far from blameless for the conditions in which many working-class families existed. Women were regularly described as particularly debauched, lazy, and spendthrift, drinking with their husbands, taking lovers, and prostituting themselves.[21] It was women's supposed taste for excess that contributed to the economic misery of the working class family, as the Industrial Society of Mulhouse implied in 1878:

> We regret the excess of women, and especially of young girls, who spend the better part of their wages on luxury clothing, and especially on hairstyles. In the past they wore little bonnets with modest ribbons; now each girl wants to adorn herself with flowers, and in her heart of hearts probably wishes she were wearing a work-of-art made out of fake hair....We also regret that working-class women have abandoned cotton dresses, sturdy and easy to wash, to buy instead these half-cotton little fabrics of inferior quality, that do not last long and cannot be washed well....It would be wiser, on the part of the working father of the family, to be content with less expensive clothing on holidays, and to devote the money he thus saved to the education of his children.[22]

Excess and overindulgence were thought to characterize not only workers' consumption habits, but their sexual behavior. Concerns about night work revolved around the assumption that workers' moral structure was so weak that even simple social contact, especially at night, could lead to sexual liaisons.[23] Even within the family, workers were understood as sexualized beings. One of the most prominent explanations given for working-class poverty was the *fecondité*, or fertility, of the working class, and in particular, its "exuberant and bestial fertility."[24] In the lexicon of *la question sociale*, this supposedly rampant sexual activity was coupled with a damaging love of alcohol and gambling, all of which could be explained by workers' general lack of moderation and restraint.[25] Their lack of restraint and their tendency to ignore the future consequences of their actions were regularly attributed to workers' immaturity and their inability to care for themselves. Industrialists' descriptions of working-class behavior often assumed the tone of parents despairing of their children's misbehavior, and frustrated with their stubbornness and ignorance. This frustration was clear in the mayor of Mulhouse's lament about workers' refusal to take good advice on keeping their homes clean and healthy. "What can authorities do in private homes?" he wrote to the Prefect in 1829. "Give advice, distribute disinfectants? But we can neither force them to open their windows, nor oblige them to employ the medications we give them, which are probably sold if they have any value, or thrown out."[26]

Given their early disclosure of *la question sociale*, it is not surprising that French industrialists also proposed one of the earliest, and most influential, solutions. That solution was paternalism, a form of labor management in which social relations between employers and employees were deemed analogous to the relationship between a father and his children, with benevolent assistance and protection offered in exchange for deferential obedience and loyalty. Industrial paternalism usually took the form of efforts to build housing for workers[27]; to offer educational opportunities[28]; to organize health services[29]; to administer a variety of pension plans, insurance programs, and savings accounts[30]; to provide instruction in housekeeping and child-care skills[31]; and to organize leisure-time activities.[32] Paternalism generally developed in what one economic historian refers to as the *France du développement*: the France that lay east of an imaginary line running from Cherbourg in the northwest to Marseille in the southeast.[33] The best-known paternalist firms of the nineteenth century—the collieries of the North, the steel mills of the Lorraine and the Saône-et-Loire, and the textile mills of Alsace—lay in this industrially developed sector. It was because paternalism and prestigious firms went hand-in-hand that paternalism, although never the dominant industrial policy practiced by manufacturers, was the best-known. By the mid-nineteenth century, paternalism had become an important feature of the industrial landscape, and the problems it was designed to solve had captured the attentions, and raised the anxieties, of a wide public.[34] But paternalism was also a solution to *la question sociale* that derived from the central preoccupation of industrialists as they observed and described their workers and their problems. If, as so many industrialists believed, workers lacked the self-control and foresight necessary to operate successfully in an industrial economy; if they were unprepared, or inadequately prepared, to shoulder the responsibility for proper behavior, whether on the job or at home; if they were, in short, *undisciplined*, then the appropriate solution for workers' misery, at least in the short term, was a solution that emulated parental care, that substituted help by industrialists for self-help. For French industrialists grappling with *la question sociale*, industrial prosperity seemed to demand an involvement in workers' public and private lives with an eye both to mitigating the human costs of industrialization and maintaining profits.

At an 1866 meeting of the Industrial Society of Mulhouse, Frederick Engel-Dollfus, a well-known Alsatian industrialist, explained the rationale behind Mulhousian industrialists' adoption of paternalist projects:

> The manufacturer owes something more to his workers than a salary; it is equally his obligation to concern himself with their moral and physical condition, and this obligation, which no type of salary can replace, must take precedence over considerations of private interest.[35]

Despite these common and frequent expressions of humanitarianism, industrialists never hid the economic motives behind their paternalist projects. In reports to its general assemblies, the *Compagnie des mines de houille de Blanzy*, a mining firm in the Saône-et-Loire, often attributed its paternalist projects to the need to attract workers to an otherwise unattractive industry.[36] Helping workers was a step toward assuring industrial success, as the steel firm *Établissements Schneider* made quite explicit in a report given to the French Chamber of Deputies:

> In working for the well-being of the working class...one is not only satisfying an obligation toward humanity, one is also acting wisely in the interest of industry. It has been demonstrated that it is an important element of success for a factory to give its workers a salary which permits them to provide for all their needs, to develop their intelligence and their morality, and to win their confidence and their loyalty....Without moralization, one cannot obtain a constant, regular and devoted labor force. Without education, one can neither form elite workers for different types of work, nor even ordinary laborers.[37]

Like the *Compagnie des mines de houille de Blanzy*, the *Établissements Schneider* congratulated itself in 1863 on the success of its effort to create a steady and disciplined labor force. Not only was the present generation of workers educated, disciplined, and loyal, but the company's paternalist strategies had also produced a second generation of workers. The company's success was thus assured not only by the quality of its products, but by the quality and dependability of its workers.[38] Even earlier, in 1829, Alsatian industrialist Jean Zuber warned:

> Look around you. Do you see prosperity settling in the place where, from workers up to masters, everything radiates that spirit of isolation and suspicion which characterized the corporations of the last century...or instead, don't you see fortune turning toward the side where everything radiates a liberal and philanthropic spirit, where employers see it as a duty to give education and ease to their workers?[39]

The operative words here were "prosperity" and "fortune." Nothing about paternalist programs, according to Mulhousian industrialists, would harm a company's productivity or profitability. In fact, well-fed, well-housed, and well-educated workers could only improve productivity and profitability.[40] From early in the nineteenth century the manufacturing elite of Mulhouse believed that the money they spent paternalist institutions would come back to them in the form of a stable, reliable, and loyal workforce.

Industrialists were not nearly as optimistic as political economists had once been about the success of non-intervention as a method of labor management, and often accompanied their explanations of paternalism with explicit critiques of a *laissez-faire* approach to their workers. As early as the 1830s, Alsatian industrialists criticized what they perceived to be political economists' unfamiliarity with economic reality. One argued that whereas the most logical theoretical solution during a commercial crisis would be to lay off his workers and shut down his factory until the economic outlook improved, common humanity prohibited him from ignoring his workers during periods of catastrophe.[41] Manufacturers understood the misery that overproduction and economic crises caused among workers, and pointed out that if economists studied actual economic conditions rather than holding tight to their absolute and unchanging natural laws, they would realize that although overproduction should have been a theoretical impossibility, it unfortunately was a practical reality.[42] The *Bulletin de la Société Industrielle de Mulhouse* argued that:

> These economists are very calm in the presence of these facts, thinking that overproduction will correct itself by either ceasing or diminishing production for a period of time. They wait patiently for the surplus to be sold. From the inside of their offices this situation is clear and simple enough, but in the presence of reality itself, what evil, what suffering, until this equilibrium is reestablished.[43]

Even when industrialists offered no explicit critiques of *laissez-faire* economic principles, they recognized that the industrial capitalist economy did not necessarily operate in the neat, predictable manner described in political economic theory, and that industrialization had had unforeseen and unfortunate consequences, not only for workers, but for themselves. French departmental archives are filled with letters from industrialists to local officials complaining of economic crises, unemployed workers, the need to support these workers on municipal funds, and the threat of social violence looming above industrial towns.[44] Whether the industrialists of towns like Mulhouse or Le Creusot really had anything to fear from their workers, it is nonetheless significant that industrialists in these towns clearly thought that they did. They knew that they were operating in the middle of a large working-class population, outnumbered dramatically. They knew that workers lived in unsatisfactory conditions, and were well aware of what a miserable and angry working class could do, having already experienced strikes, riots, and demonstrations. Under these conditions, to rely on *laissez-faire* labor strategies that offered too little control over undisciplined workers seemed to many industrialists to be a misguided and dangerous strategy.

The Creative Powers of Paternalist Discipline

For anyone familiar with the work of Michel Foucault, the questions that nineteenth-century French industrialists were asking themselves about their undisciplined and unreliable workers appear to be (anachronistically, of course) quintessentially Foucauldian questions. What should workers be like in the factory, as employees? How should workers behave at home, in their private lives? And, how were industrialists to discipline workers into wanting to be disciplined, productive, and obedient workers at work, and moral, thrifty, and self-disciplined at home? Long before Michel Foucault wrote of the productive power of discipline, political economist Louis Reybaud, describing the textile town of Villeneuvette in 1865, wrote of the "gentle violence" of industrial paternalism:

> The secret of its strength is that the boss is motivated by good intentions, which are so obvious that they disarm even those who believe themselves to be the most injured. Its foundation is a paternal government which imposes itself on the worker in his interest, and intends to lead him to well-being by exercising a gentle violence upon him.[45]

As Reybaud suggested, to argue that paternalism only represses is to ignore what is both novel and interesting about it. To examine paternalism as a creative system of power is to employ Michel Foucault's definition of power not as repressive, but as productive.[46] To argue that the effectiveness of paternalism lay in its gentleness rather than in its violence, that it *created* potentialities, capabilities, and capacities, allows the historian to see how industrial paternalism attempted to create discipline out of indiscipline, or docile, mute, productive, stable, and moral bodies out of supposedly disobedient, unproductive, and immoral ones.

Paternalist efforts, then, were examples of what Foucault referred to as disciplinary technology. It was in his work on the prison that Foucault most closely examined the operations of disciplinary technology: the efforts to turn the individual into a body that could be controlled, molded, regulated, managed, and normalized.[47] In the nineteenth century, however, disciplinary technology could also be found operating in schools, in armies, in factories, and most certainly, in the paternalist factory town, and the agents of disciplinary technology were teachers, generals, prison wardens, as well as factory owners. Paraphrasing Hubert Dreyfus and Paul Rabinow's analysis, discipline works on the body and treats the body as an object to be molded into something more obedient and more skillful; it works through controlling the space and time that a body inhabits, as well as the motions that a particular body can make; and it works through a constant surveillance—or an impression of surveillance—of the body/bodies, that is, a population.[48]

According to Foucault, however, discipline not only constructs individuals as the *objects* of disciplinary technology, but also individuals who become the self-regulating *subjects* enforcing and embodying disciplinary technology.[49] While technologies of discipline create docile and productive bodies, they also create subjects who self-discipline. Paternalist practices were sites of discipline, of creating obedient, productive, and docile workers out of undisciplined ones; but they were also sites for creating workers who had taken upon themselves the idea that they *ought* to be obedient to their bosses, that they *ought* to be at work on time, that they *ought* not to question their employers or undermine the productivity of the work routine. Industrial paternalism set the standards, the norms, the rules; docile, productive, disciplined, obedient bodies were created; but those bodies/subjects were then left the task of continuing the process of self-discipline, self-regulation, self-normalization, and, more significantly, of seeing and understanding the benefits of continuing this process.

If, as Louis Reybaud wrote, industrial paternalism was a process of industrialists leading workers "to well-being by exercising a gentle violence upon [them]," then what was this hypothetical well-being supposed to look like? What were the norms to which a "disciplined" working class would conform? Two competitions organized in 1864 and 1874 by the Industrial Society of Mulhouse for workers living in the city's housing projects, or *cités ouvrières,* offer a quick snapshot of the disciplined nature of the working class that paternalist efforts were designed to produce or at least encourage. The 1874 competition, known officially as the *Prix Salathé pour l'encouragement de la classe ouvrière à l'économie* [Prize for the Encouragement of Economy among the Working Class], was designed to "encourage the spirit of thrift and to further family sentiments."[50] To be considered a candidate for the prize, which consisted of 400 francs to be used to purchase a home in the *cité ouvrière*, a worker (male) had to be married, be younger than thirty-five, have given proof of household order [*ordre dans son ménage*], hard work, and good conduct, have worked for the same employer for at least three successive years, have a savings of 150-200 francs per year, and finally, not own a home. The 1864 competition went so far as to describe the criteria on which judges would rank contestants: the general order and cleanliness of both the interior and exterior of homes, the condition of furniture, the condition of gardens, the order and thrift of the household, the care of children and their attendance at school, and the wages of family members.

These two competitions suggest that the discipline so urgently sought by industrialists was broadly understood and took a variety of forms. Industrialists wanted workers who were hard-working, obedient, and docile, and who followed orders. But they also wanted a working class that was physically stable, that did not move from season to season, and that was exclusively committed to industrial work rather than to a combination of agricultural and industrial work. Ideally, they wanted workers who would join the firm at a young age, work until retirement, and remain loyal and devoted employees throughout their lives.[51] The techniques designed to operationalize this desire for discipline, loyalty, and stability were, then, some of the key features of the paternalist factory town: the school system that taught students discipline and allegiance to the firm even as it taught them to read and write; the housing that offered workers a place to call their own, tying workers to the firm and the town, and thus discouraging the use of industrial work as temporary or seasonal employment; the benefits that gave workers something to lose if they left, or were forced to leave, the firm.

While paternalism was intended to shift the relationship between employers and employees away from one based on wages to one based on loyalty and discipline, employers also appeared to be trying to create employees rather than workers.[52] This was particularly evident in Le Creusot, with its complicated educational system and its attempts to move qualified workers through the employment hierarchy into positions of added responsibility.[53] But it was also evident in certain Mulhousian textile firms. The firm of J.-J. Bourcart in Guebwiller, for instance, tended to hire its foremen and other employees from among those men who participated regularly in the firm's schools, library societies and discussion groups.[54] In other words, it appears that industrialists recognized that workers who were self-motivated members of the industrial enterprise would be more useful and productive than workers who had to be repeatedly coerced into following orders.

The construction of housing was usually the first effort made by paternalist industrialists to assist and discipline their workers. Industrialists regularly discussed not only the value of providing workers with housing, but also the actual construction of homes: whether or not they should be single-family homes, how many single-family homes could be safely placed side-by-side, where to place the kitchen in relation to the bedroom, and how to prevent the destruction and misuse of the property. These discussions reflect the complex web of attributes that industrialists hoped the carefully structured and organized home would help workers adopt. Many assumed that homes would stabilize families, make it possible to have large families, and improve the hygiene of living conditions, thereby reducing the death rate among newborns, increasing the life-span of adult workers, and improving the general health and strength of all workers. Not only, however, did industrialists want numbers of workers, they also wanted moral, monogamous, and stable workers. Homes in which living and sleeping areas were separated, in which parents and children were separated, in which cooking was separated from all other areas, homes with no dark, cramped areas that could breed disease, whether actual physical disease or moral disease: these appeared to be the instruments by which to assure the desired worker. With this in mind, industrialists closely regulated what could and could not be done in company housing. In many towns, workers were forbidden to take in lodgers, or to rent rooms to other families; they were also forbidden to repaint or remodel their homes, to keep animals inside the home, or to use the garden space for anything other than growing flowers and vegetables.[55] And despite industrialists' touting of the benefits of private property for workers, working-class homes were anything but private. The regulations of the *cité ouvrière* in Montceau-les-Mines gave administrators of the firm the right to enter workers' homes at any time, day or night.[56] Similarly, the *Établissements Schneider* kept meticulous records about the private lives of workers: workers who failed to pay rent, workers who kept pets, workers who were married or unmarried, the numbers of unmarried women and widows living in company property, workers who kept their homes in bad condition, and workers who did not live in company housing.[57]

The emphasis industrialists placed on the carefully structured and regulated working-class home suggests that they wanted workers' private lives to center around the home rather than around other centers of working-class sociability, like the ubiquitous café, and around the family rather than around large groups of workers. The café, and the frequency with which male workers visited the café, was one of the most frequently cited causes of what industrialists perceived to be a breakdown of family relations among industrial workers. Industrialists generally attributed workers' enjoyment of café life to their squalid living conditions, and suggested that pleasant and roomy homes of which workers could be proud might keep workers with their families rather than out gallivanting in cafés.

Cafés were also assumed to attract large numbers of workers, a source of fear during the nineteenth century, and a sign of revolutionary potential. In order to create family life and reduce the potential for transmitting revolutionary ideas and simple protest, industrialists believed that workers had to be moved out of the café where large numbers of workers congregated to socialize, and out of crowded working-class slums, where vices could be transmitted like contagious diseases.[58] In a 1907 report about the Mulhousian *cités ouvrières*, an observer wrote that the "inconveniences" that often resulted from workers living too closely together had been eliminated in Mulhouse by creating single-family dwellings lined up side-by-side and sharing only one wall (rather than one home on top of another in the same building), each with its own entrance.[59]

Linked to the creation of a wholesome, family-oriented working-class home life was the replacement of traditional working-class forms of recreation with something else. Industrialists considered the café not only as the substitute home or place of sociability for most workers, but also their primary form of recreation. The café was therefore precisely the locus of working-class recreation the industrial bourgeoisie wanted to discourage. This desire is clearly revealed in industrialists' efforts to provide their workers with gardens and with other "moral" leisure-time pursuits:

> The man who in the past had spent all of the time he could outside of his home and probably in the bar because his home, too small and badly cared-for, lacked appeal for him, today loves to cultivate his little garden, to follow the progress of his plants, to contribute to the good upkeep of his house, and thus finds his sweetest pleasures in the middle of the family that shares them.[60]

According to industrialists, gardens could teach workers the benefits of private property, hard work, and foresight. By providing produce, gardens would cut down on the wages employers had to pay, stretch workers' wages further, and discourage drinking and the frequenting of cafés. Finally, gardening, as a family or individual pursuit, would cut down on collective socializing between workers.[61] Industrialists' efforts at encouraging workers' property ownership—in the form of a house and garden—also reveal that thrift was another critical trait of the ideal disciplined working class. Industrialists hoped that property ownership would instill in workers a desire to spend carefully, save money, and plan for the future. To this end, certain employers paid their workers on a monthly rather than biweekly basis in an effort to force them to save money.[62]

While paternalist projects were the sites of efforts to create disciplined bodies (physically-disciplined; thrifty; industrious, self-controlled), moral bodies (paternal/maternal toward children; monogamous; temperate), and docile bodies (loyal to the firm; obedient of rules; unquestioning of the status quo), they were also sites of efforts to create politically acquiescent bodies. Behind paternalist projects was a concern to change supposedly politically radical workers into politically conservative, or even better, quiescent, ones: workers who acted as "good" citizens and respected laws; workers who understood themselves as members of society rather than outsiders to civil and political society; workers who, if they did not vote exactly the way their employers did, at least exercised their right to vote in a peaceful, non-disruptive manner, preferably voting for non-socialist and therefore non-threatening candidates.[63] Industrial firms sometimes implied that both ownership of private property and education would have significant effects on the citizenship qualities and voting habits of workers. In a company pamphlet written in 1867, for instance, the *Compagnie des mines de houille de Blanzy* wrote that "the worker raised as an owner of private property becomes thrifty and orderly; he works courageously and abandons the cabarets; from this day forth, society has acquired one more friend of order."[64]

These traits of the "disciplined" working class appear surprisingly similar to a "bourgeois" ethic or morality: a glorification of industriousness, thrift, foresight, self-control, reason, monogamy, legitimate marriage, a private family life, and love of children. Paternalist discipline and its objectifying as well as subjectifying effects were bound up with universalizing a particularly bourgeois ethic on behalf of the working class. Hard work, discipline, thrift, morality—all these were key attributes of the nineteenth-century French bourgeoisie anxious to define itself both against the aristocracy and the working class. But these bourgeois norms were presented as a universal ethic, as an ethos applicable not simply to the bourgeoisie, but to the working class as well.[65] It is in this universalization of a bourgeois ethic that one can truly see the subjectifying impulse within paternalism. Docile, productive, disciplined, and obedient bodies could have been created through repression: clear standards, precise rules, harsh punishments for infractions. But what industrial paternalism demonstrated was a more pronounced desire to turn over the task of discipline to workers themselves, to encourage workers to *want* to self-regulate and self-discipline, to encourage the formation of self-identities for which self-discipline was natural, normal, and advantageous. Paternalist discipline was intended to make individuals who understood themselves *not* as people who had been, and were being, disciplined, but as individuals who had chosen to self-discipline and self-regulate because of the benefits that accrued to this type of behavior, benefits proven by the success of the French bourgeoisie.

No archival record exists of the name or the winning qualifications of the Mulhousian textile worker who collected the 1874 *Prix Salathé pour l'encouragement de la classe ouvrière à l'économie.* And yet it would be surprising had the winning worker been anyone but someone who embodied the broad understanding of discipline situated at the core of industrial paternalism. For many French industrialists, allowing their undisciplined and unruly workers to ameliorate their own misery, as economic theory suggested they should, was a dangerously risky tactic. If industrial factory labor appeared to render workers more miserable and thus less disciplined, paternalism entailed strategies that appeared to render workers less miserable and thus more disciplined. The winner of the *Prix Salathé* was almost certainly someone who was not only more regulated, managed, controlled, and normalized, but someone capable of self-regulation, self-management, self-control. It was through the twin techniques of discipline and self-discipline that French industrialists hoped to address *la question sociale* and alleviate, if not eradicate, the problem of social misery.

Political Economy and the Advocacy of Paternalism

What is particularly significant about industrialists' early and direct encounter with *la question social,* and their implementation of paternalism as an appropriate solution, was that they wrote publicly about both. The industrial families of paternalist towns like Mulhouse, Montceau-les-Mines, and Le Creusot, to name only some of the best known, published an abundant variety of pamphlets, books, tables, graphs, and photographs, describing the paternalist institutions and services offered by the firms to their employees.[66] Particularly influential was the *Bulletin de la Société Industrielle de Mulhouse,* published for the first time in 1828 by the Industrial Society of Mulhouse, which, although primarily devoted to technical discussions, was also an important vehicle for Mulhousian industrialists' discussions of labor, labor management, and the problems of the working class. Later in the century, the industrial dynasties of Mulhouse, Le Creusot, and Montceau-les-Mines participated in the 1867, 1889, and 1900 World's Fairs, providing exhibits on their paternalist strategies, and regularly winning prizes for their efforts.

Foremost among the wide public that paid careful and respectful attention to industrialists were French political economists. Faced with the unexpected *question sociale,* and familiar with the paternalism of France's more significant factory towns, by the mid-nineteenth century political economists became relentless publicists and advocates of paternalism. Like industrialists, whose work they read and whose policies they studied, political economists asserted that with improved material conditions for workers—clean homes, decent clothes, sufficient food, heat—would come a new commitment to hard work and domestic order, as well as a new respect for the law and the economic organization of society.[67] Most important, improved material conditions would give workers the sense of human dignity that spawned all self-improvement.[68] And since workers could not improve their material and moral conditions without help, who better than manufacturers, therefore, to provide this assistance?

> When a vice has laid deep roots in an entire social class, that vice cannot be eliminated without prodigious efforts, and this class itself, exhausted by this vice, will certainly not have the necessary energy to take the initiative for a change and a reform. It is necessary, therefore, that the impulse should come from elsewhere, from the superior classes, and especially from masters and entrepreneurs.[69]

And what better way for manufacturers to help workers than to remember the social links that bound them to their workers, links that transcended the impersonal wage contract and ought never to be forgotten?[70] As political economist Henri Baudrillart succinctly wrote:

> Lots of benevolence, not inefficient and cold, but active and reconcilable with authority, a responsibility which feels itself to be entrusted with souls—this is what we need to ask not just from several industrialists, but from all.[71]

By the mid-nineteenth century, then, the pages of the *Journal des économistes* were filled with discussions of manufacturers' housing projects, savings accounts, gardens, and housekeeping schools. Like industrialists, political economists emphasized the economic as well as the social benefits of paternalist labor management strategies. Manufacturers were mistaken, Louis-René Villermé argued, if they thought that miserable workers would make good workers:

> And what to say about the indifference of those masters who never have a word of encouragement for their workers, who never see them outside the workshops, who never address a single word to them, who only respond to their questions with a hard or offensive monosyllable, and who have pushed the naiveté of their egoism to the point of admitting to me that in the interest of the worker himself, it was good for him always to be in the grasp of poverty, because that way, they said to me, he would not be a bad example to his children, and his misery would guarantee his good behavior.[72]

Instead, material comfort, stability, and security would inspire hard work and loyalty on the part of workers and assure domestic harmony within the working-class family. And well-organized and happy working-class families, economists argued, would ensure social peace as well as economic prosperity.[73]

Given what paternalism was, however—a technique of discipline and control, a productive or creative interventionist strategy, a form of gentle violence—it represented a disciplinary problem for political economy. Self-professed scientists, political economists—unlike industrialists—not only had to offer an explanation for *la question sociale* and working-class misery, but also an explanation and justification for the paternalist solution they now proposed and advocated. In 1842, economist Jerome Adolphe Blanqui bravely and decisively announced that free trade had caused nothing but misery for French workers:

> To this day, experience has invalidated only one of Adam Smith's doctrines. I am talking about the one which attributes to absolute freedom of industry the ability to provide all social necessities and the possibility of realizing all types of progress....Since then we have seen that the natural course of things produces disastrous effects, and creates anarchy in production, wars for opportunities and piracy in competition. The division of labor and the improvement of machines, which were supposed to have secured some leisure for the working-class family....have only engendered exhaustion and misery.[74]

His colleagues did not always share Blanqui's certainty, however. Unlike Blanqui, most political economists seem instead to have been fundamentally unsure—as evidenced by their vacillation—as to the cause of *la question sociale*. Villermé, for instance, was clearly hesitant about how to explain working-class misery, and concluded his *Tableau de l'état physique et moral des ouvriers* with reference to everything from workers' behavior to capitalist crises:

> workers in factories lack sobriety, thrift, foresight, morals, and very often it is their own fault if they are miserable. This evil is not new, but it is now greater than ever. It results primarily from the regular gathering of workers in large workshops, sorts of caravansaries, where those of different sexes and different ages find themselves mixed together, and from their living in cities, which industry multiplies by creating agglomerations of population. It also comes from free competition, this cause of the expansion, of the prodigious development which industry has achieved, but also from the frequent overproduction of manufactured goods, from the cluttering of stores, from the depreciation of merchandise, from the ruin of the large number of manufacturers, and from many crises, from many oscillations in the wage rate, which are so harmful to workers.[75]

More succinctly, Théodore Fix argued that *la question sociale* had three causes: workers' immorality, employers' immorality, and (significantly) the very condition of being a worker.[76]

However ambiguously political economists explained *la question sociale*, by mid-century it was the lone voice who argued either that *la question sociale* was a temporary problem and thus that nothing should be done except to wait until the naturally balanced laws of the economy corrected the situation, or that if workers were intent upon behaving badly, they should be left alone to suffer the consequences. Even as they continued to dispute the argument that political economy was an immoral science, economists began to acknowledge that they had left "man" out of their economic formulae, thus dehumanizing their science. "Wealth no longer produces itself, man produces it," economist Henri Baudrillart wrote in 1864; "it no longer distributes itself, man divides it under the conditions of certain laws; labor no longer divides itself, man divides it. It is the mechanical nature of these expressions...which tend to make a science of things out of a science of humanity."[77] Modern poverty, economist Antoine Cherbuliez argued, had created a class of people who had been stripped of their humanity, and the consequences, if only in terms of sheer numbers of dehumanized men and women, were profound:

> Once the poor man begins to lose his dignity as a free man and an honest worker, he can no longer get up, and begins to fall even lower...he falls, in short, into bestiality, and finishes by no longer having any sense of his abasement or his destitution. This is the condition today of more than a million and a half Irish peasants; this is the condition of workers who inhabit the neighborhoods of towns like London,

Liverpool, Manchester and Leeds in England, and of Lille, Rouen and Lyon in France.[78]

In short, by the mid-nineteenth century, political economists had begun to argue that the causes of *la question sociale* were complex and multi-dimensional, and that while workers may have contributed to their own misery, neither the French state nor the French economy could afford to rely exclusively upon *laissez-faire* as a corrective when it came to human resources.

It was this recognition—that flesh-and-blood human beings lay behind the category of Labor, and that these flesh-and-blood human beings, suffering and miserable, needed to be assisted not simply for moral reasons, but because they constituted a human resource that could not be wasted or destroyed—that situates the history of nineteenth-century French political economy squarely in the larger history of what Michel Foucault labeled "governmentality" and its entwined relationship with the human sciences. Governmentality refers to the recognition that human populations are a resource, and thus a problem of state.[79] It is a realization that Foucault dated from the seventeenth century, when the European population's improved conditions, and thus its longer life-span, entailed the insight by those in power that the population could be *used* productively, and thus should be properly managed, shaped, controlled, and modified. Keeping the population alive, helping it to live longer, encouraging it to be more productive: these concerns now appeared to be issues of state.

Through its participation in discussions of *la question sociale* and its paternalist solution, political economy was thus complicit in a general social anxiety about populations, and in particular, about the working majority of that population. Economists' concern with *la question sociale* emerged from their realization that miserable, sick, underfed people could not contribute to the strength of a state and the stability and productivity of an economy in the way that happy, healthy, well-fed people could. Louis Reybaud's introductory essay to the first volume of the *Journal des économistes*, with which this chapter began, can thus be read as an acknowledgment of the problem of governmentality. It was a statement that recognized the resources represented by a population and acknowledged the inability of political economy to thus far properly include this population and its problems into its science.

Political economy was but one of many nineteenth-century human sciences concerned with the health and vitality of populations, complicit in the collection of knowledge about the human resources of the state, and thus bound up in an intertwined relationship between power and knowledge.[80]

Nineteenth-century political economy can just as effectively illuminate the workings of power/knowledge as Foucault's celebrated work on the medical profession and the medical examination.[81] Just as the medical profession specialized in the examination of ill patients, so did the academic discipline of political economy specialize in the examination of Labor, and of the relationship between the economy and Labor. Political economy's "gaze" upon workers created knowledge: about what happened when unemployment grew; or when prices rose and wages did not; or when the state implemented either protectionist or free trade policies; or when workers suffered from a lack of resources. But that gaze also generated power: to define workers as individuals capable of caring for themselves or as inherently in need of outside assistance; to depict the industrialist capitalist economy as one beneficial to all social groups or as intrinsically inequitable; to portray the process of "pulling oneself up by one's bootstraps" as open to all or as class-specific; and to influence laws, policies, and regulations based upon the above assumptions. In short, political economy produced knowledge about populations, knowledge that the state could use if it were going to manage the longevity, health, and productivity of the population.

Foucault understood governmentality as having two poles—control of the body (or the individual) and control of the species (or the population)—which came together in the nineteenth-century preoccupation with sex.[82] But those two poles also came together in the nineteenth-century preoccupation with *la question sociale*. The social question explicitly linked the vitality of the individual body with the vitality of the human species, and in political economy's concern with *la question sociale* one can see a concern not only with what would happen to individual workers should their miseries be ignored, but what would happen to the human species, and in particular, to the majority of the species who worked. If people were a resource, they were now of interest not simply to the state, but to political economists, who studied the economic resources of the state. *La question sociale*, then, was the realization that how people worked, lived, and died mattered, not just for moral reasons, but for economic reasons; that everyday activities of living, dying, working, being miserable or being happy, were economically significant.[83]

Several warnings made by Foucauldian scholars apply, however, to the relationship between political economy, *la question sociale*, and governmentality. It would be a mistake to see the state masterminding every effort to improve the health of a population, whether that was to improve the public hygiene in the city of Paris, the medical care available to French citizens, or, in the case of political economists, the material conditions of the French working class. It would also be a mistake, not to mention overly-simplistic, to see the efforts of psychiatry, social work, and public hygiene, to name just a few human sciences, as all necessarily complicit in fulfilling the needs of the state, and thus as all engaging in efforts to control and shape populations. Every psychiatrist is not a servant of the state; every social worker is not "disciplining" or "normalizing" his or her clients; every doctor is not collecting information on behalf of the state when he or she performs an examination of a patient.[84] Instead, as Foucault argued:

> Power relations are both intentional and nonsubjective. If in fact they are intelligible, this is not because they are the effect of another instance that "explains" them, but rather because they are imbued, through and through, with calculation: there is no power that is exercised without a series of aims and objectives. But this does not mean that it results from the choice or decision of an individual subject; let us not look for the headquarters that presides over its rationality; neither the caste which governs, nor the groups which control the state apparatus, nor those who make the most important economic decisions direct the entire network of power that functions in a society (and makes *it* function);[85]

Or, more succinctly, "people know what they do; they frequently know why they do what they do; but what they don't know is what what they do does."[86]

These warnings, however, point to a significant difference between political economy and other human sciences such as psychiatry, medicine, and social work. What cannot be attributed to all human scientists—that doctors examining their patients or psychiatrists analyzing their clients were ultimately concerned with the vitality of the larger population—*can*, in fact, be attributed to nineteenth-century economists. Unlike doctors, psychiatrists, and social workers, political economists explicitly claimed to be interested in the health, longevity, and productivity of the population. Given that economists saw populations as a resource, economists, by definition, *had* to be interested in the health of those populations. Despite political economy's championing of the principle of *laissez-faire*, the discipline originated—as nineteenth-century French political economists would have acknowledged—with a concern for the "wealth of nations." Even the most conservative French economists, those most committed to *laissez-faire*, would have argued that *laissez-faire* was crucial, not just as an abstract principle, but as a means to an end, that end being a strong, healthy, economically-viable state.

If economists were more explicitly concerned with the vitality and productivity of human resources than were other human scientists, discipline also meant something far more concrete for political economists than it did for doctors, psychiatrists, or social workers. Whereas it is inappropriate to see an explicit project of social discipline behind every practitioner of social work, it would be less inappropriate to see that project behind political economists' discussions of *la question sociale* and their support of paternalism. This claim is not to ignore the warnings elaborated above; it is not to argue that all political economists were acting as servants of the state when they advocated paternalism, or that it was only discipline and obedience (rather than a sincerely compassionate alleviation of hunger, illness, and early death) that economists envisioned as the consequence of paternalism. It is, however, to recognize that social aggregates—populations and their vitality, longevity, and productivity—mattered explicitly as a category of analysis to economists. Given what political economists claimed as their proper arena of study; given the topics in which they claimed expertise; given the natural laws that they claim to have uncovered, it seems only reasonable that political economists would have been interested in the health, vitality, productivity (read: discipline), and longevity of the population. Hence their participation in discussions of *la question sociale*; hence their sense that something needed to be done to ameliorate the worst excesses of industrial capitalism; and hence their belief that paternalism represented the best possible solution to the problem of social misery.

But to solve *la question sociale* implied intervention into the most private recesses of workers' lives; to implement paternalism entailed control. In short, under the pressures of *la question sociale*, French political economists confronted the exigencies of *government*.[87] By mid-century, faced with the realities of social misery, and fearful of the long-term ramifications of that misery, economists began to argue that staying out of workers' lives might, in fact, represent a dangerous strategy; that solving *la question sociale* might require the direction, management, correction, discipline, and regulation of workers' lives. Regulation, direction, and management, however, and the intervention and control that they implied, made economists nervous. According to the tenets of nineteenth-century political economy, regulation was something that happened naturally, through the inherently harmonious and balanced laws of the economy. Control was exercised by the individual on his or her own behalf, not by someone or something on someone else's behalf. Discipline and correction were self-taught individual attributes. Government—

shaping the conduct of workers through the objectifying and subjectifying practices of discipline—thus appeared to undermine the fundamental *laissez-faire* tenet of political economy, the tenet upon which economists rested their claim to scientific authority. What would discipline (the paternalist solution to *la question sociale*) thus mean for their discipline (political economy)?

In short, facing French economists by the mid-nineteenth century was the dangerous challenge that *la question sociale* and its paternalist solution posed to the new science of political economy: the challenge of how to graft government onto their science. By mid-century, political economy's gaze upon workers had revealed knowledge that did not fit its scientific framework and that threatened the power and authority to interpret that knowledge that economists claimed for themselves. How that unwanted information forced shifts within the science of political economy in order to protect its claims to legitimately observe its subjects, create knowledge, and then interpret and implement that knowledge, is the story that the next chapter tells.

3. The Invention of Social Economy

By the mid-nineteenth century political economists recognized that the scientific coherence, and hence the status, of political economy was under attack. *La question sociale* had demonstrated that political economy was less like the natural sciences of physics, chemistry, and mathematics than economists had once presumed. By the publication of the first volume of the *Journal des économistes* in 1841, one senses among economists a growing unease with their earlier confidence in the predictive abilities of their science, a growing confusion about the veracity of their supposedly natural and universal theorems, and a mounting discomfort with their earlier assessment of the causes of working-class misery. If *la question sociale* was a malfunction in, and thus a challenge to, the natural harmony and self-correction of economic laws, political economists' proposed solution to working-class misery—paternalism—was an unmistakable intervention into the private lives of workers and thus a clear contradiction of the foundational disciplinary tenet that asserted that individuals should be left alone to make their own decisions. French political economists understood, then, that they needed to be able to explain *la question sociale*, to explain why their science's blueprint for the economic mechanisms of society was not working in practice the way it was supposed to. And they recognized that they were going to have to graft paternalism onto their science in such a way that the fundamental assumptions of political economy were not harmed, its claim to scientific authority not weakened, and its institutional ambitions not undermined.

This chapter investigates political economists' efforts to solve both the disciplinary and institutional problems caused for their science by their encounter with the unexpected and unwelcome *question sociale*. It examines the odd category of *économie sociale*, or social economy, that began to appear in economists' writing at the same time as their encounter with *la question sociale*. Social economy offered political economists a space—conveniently proximal yet sufficiently distant—to house everything that did not fit into their narrowly-defined and inflexible science. As nineteenth-century French economists discussed the anomaly of *la question sociale*—and as they slowly invented the new category of social economy to hold this anomaly—they tried to ascertain what the disciplinary relationship was between political and social economy, what they were doing, in other words, when they spoke not of Labor and *laissez-faire,* but of workers, their misery, and the best way to mitigate that misery. In their discussions of *la question sociale,* one perceives economists' efforts to grapple with the questions lying at the heart of their mid-century dilemma: how would their discipline be affected by a new emphasis on the consequences of industrialization, and in particular, by their advocacy of paternalist management strategies? How would political economy's self-declared status as a science with "universal laws" have to change? How would the discipline have to refashion the relationships it had originally posited between the state and the individual, employer and employee, bourgeois and worker? How could political economists re-discipline their discipline, harnessing everything that had escaped the narrow disciplinary framework of political economy and re-grafting it onto their self-proclaimed science, thus neutralizing the disciplinary vulnerability caused by *la question sociale*?

Political economy's vulnerability to the implications of *la question sociale* continues to tie the history of the economic discipline to the larger history of the nineteenth-century professions and human sciences. Every discipline or profession encounters problems it cannot perfectly explain, or what sociologist Andrew Abbott refers to as "crucial anomalies."[1] For Abbott, though, it is the abstraction of the knowledge system that lies behind any profession, whether academic or not, that offers a means of confronting the challenges a profession constantly faces. It is the theoretical nature of any profession's knowledge system that allows that profession to deal with circumstances that threaten to undermine either the institutional status and power of the profession, or the power of the profession's knowledge system itself to diagnose and treat a problem. When the power of a profession's knowledge system fails, the solution is to define old problems in new ways, to use the esoteric system of abstract knowledge to re-identify problems, to re-label them, and to re-conceptualize them.

In the case of political economy, it was this ability to define old problems in new ways that allowed it to overcome the challenge posed by *la question sociale.* The creation of *économie sociale* as a new abstract category that could house *la question sociale* and all its attendant problems—everything that could not be easily fit into the framework of political economy—afforded protection to the borders that political economy had originally marked out for itself, the borders that defined it as a science that rested upon the precept of *laissez-faire.* Social economy gave economists a means of splitting off the government of human subjects, which was the responsibility of social economy, from the study of natural laws, the responsibility of political economy. Social economy offered a means, in other words, for political economy to self-discipline, to manage the unruly elements of its field of study, and control the unanticipated knowledge that had escaped its disciplinary framework. For historians, examining *économie sociale* is an opportunity to study the operations of power as they were exercised by a self-titled science—political economy—that presented itself as natural, and outside human control and human interests, that is, as outside power. *Économie sociale* offers a place to see the "structural flaws and unexpected crevices"[2] in a discipline, to explore how a discipline manages those unexpected anomalies, and how it protects its borders, its authority, its scientific pretensions, and its political ambitions.

This chapter begins with economists' recognition that *la question sociale* represented a threat to the coherence of their science, and thus to their own professional ambitions. This recognition was particularly noticeable in economists' criticisms of themselves and their discipline (recall Louis Reybaud's confession in the first volume of the *Journal des économistes*), as well as in their efforts to redefine the type of science that political economy truly was, and the terrain that its jurisdiction actually covered. I then tackle the "physiognomy" of social economy: what social economy looked like in the pages of economic journals, and what types of concerns constituted the topic of social economy as understood by political economists. While nineteenth-century *économie sociale* looked remarkably standard on the page, economists consistently disagreed as to the proper definition and boundaries of their new category. Here, then, I explore the origins of the term *économie sociale*, as well as the myriad definitions of this new category offered by economists. Finally, I explore how this newly-invented category of *économie sociale* offered economists a means to protect their discipline and its scientific pretensions from the threat of *la question sociale*. I examine one particular debate that preoccupied economists during the second half of the nineteenth century, a debate over the relationship between the science and the art of political economy, to illustrate the process of border patrol that *économie sociale* allowed economists to accomplish, thereby disciplining their own discipline.

The Vulnerable Jurisdictions of Political Economy

In 1851, Honoré Frégier, an observer of the French working class, offered the following critique of French political economy:

> Political economy...has proven itself to be inadequate in the accomplishment of its own mission, because it has not wanted to leave the sphere of abstraction, and because it has only concerned itself with the economic element of a complex question—that is, economic, moral, and political at the same time—an element which without a doubt needs to be taken into consideration, but which cannot alone suffice to sketch out an essentially practical difficulty.[3]

While Frégier was not a political economist, his statements suggest the types of critiques that mid-century French political economists understood they faced. And while he was also not a member of the Ministry of Public Instruction charged with handing out educational posts, his critiques may have signaled to economists that if others agreed with his condemnation of the overly-abstract and narrowly-defined discipline of political economy, they faced challenges that might well cost them the acclaim and professional status they sought.

That challenge was recognized by Hippolyte Passy in an 1858 book review in the *Journal des économistes*. The science of political economy, he argued, had first defined its field of inquiry narrowly, focusing on the production of wealth alone. But political economy was more than just the science of wealth; it was a truly social science, and thus its field of inquiry was appropriately and quite legitimately all fields of human activity:

> But there is no social science which is free to isolate itself completely. Political economy is called upon to study phenomena which are all products of human activity; hence, the impossibility of abstaining from the examination of causes which, by operating upon human activity, determine its course and make its applications even more energetic and fecund. Taking things as they really are, political economy, like all other social sciences, is the product of a more general and noble science, a moral science...[4]

Passy's description suggests that by the mid-nineteenth century, French economists had begun to ask themselves whether the founders of the discipline had really intended political economy to be a narrow, wealth-based science, or whether it was instead a broadly based "moral" science. More and more economists were beginning to demand that the human factor be reinserted into economic formulae, and that political economy reassume some of the generosity and humanitarianism of early Enlightenment political economists. The legitimacy of these demands could be demonstrated by turning to Adam Smith's *The Wealth of Nations*, economist Henri Baudrillart argued in 1866. Had not Adam Smith himself begun his classic statement of political economy by discussing the significance of human beings in the process of production, rather than launching immediately into abstract discussions of economic laws?[5]

Of course, not all economists agreed with Fix and Passy about the state of the economic science in France. Horace Say, Jean-Baptiste Say's son, offered a much more glowing depiction of political economy in 1854:

> At no other epoch have economic studies offered as much interest as in our own. The general principles are henceforth solidly established, and the moment has come to shift the deductions into application. Already the peoples who surround France have made immense steps. The English have proven, through practice, that through commercial liberty people expand in number and in wealth. If several difficulties have arisen between what is called Labor and Capital (and it would be better to say between the different branches of Labor, since the capitalist entrepreneur of industry is a worker...), these difficulties for the most part are only tardy consequences of the unhappy systems of hindrance, of production, and of monopoly through which industry has had to pass.[6]

And yet, by 1854, Horace Say's comments had become exceptional, their quality of frantic denial hinting at an unwelcome realization that conditions had changed for the way his science operated.

Economists' skepticism reveals that by the mid-century the discipline of French political economy was moving into a phase of uncertainty and vulnerability. But whereas this uncertainty provoked anxiety and resistance among economists, many scholars have argued that vulnerability and the resultant disciplinary transformation are normal features of the historical development of academic disciplines and professions. In his analysis of the institutionalization of sociology in the French university system, for instance, Terry Clark has described the "utopian phase" through which many academic and professional disciplines pass.[7] According to Clark, a characteristic of much nineteenth-century social theory was its tendency to claim omni-explanatory power, and "to portray nothing less than the entire universe on their canvases."[8] This description of social theory's utopian phase can deservedly be applied to early nineteenth-century political economy. Although early proponents of the science had described it as a science of wealth and no more, their professed knowledge of the natural laws of the economy also implied knowledge about issues and relationships with broader social implications. Early nineteenth-century political economy was thus an odd combination of restricted scope and wide explanatory claims.[9]

But according to Clark's model, one of the main features of a mature academic discipline is the substitution of more limited claims for earlier utopian ones.[10] And again, the history of French political economy fits this model, with the addition of a small twist. The questioning of political economy's omni-explanatory claims—that industrial capitalism and *laissez-faire* could guarantee economic prosperity and social happiness for everyone; that political economy was an objective, rational, and disinterested science with universal, observable, and unchanging laws; that it could provide a blueprint for the way both society and the economy worked; and that non-intervention in the market ought to be the cardinal principle of state economic policy—manifested itself in a steady widening of the narrow and inflexible science of political economy to include subjects, explanations, and remedies that would have surprised avid supporters of classic *laissez-faire* principles. The end of political economy's utopian phase was marked, then, by an inquiry as to whether political economy was *indeed* a narrow and inflexible science of wealth, whether topics previously excluded ought not to come under the aegis of economic science, and whether claims to an explanatory power of broad social scope could be based upon political economy's supposed knowledge of a few natural economic laws.

Whereas Terry Clark uses the language of utopian versus mature phases of an academic discipline, and of limitless versus limited claims, Andrew Abbott uses the language of jurisdictions. All professions, according to Abbott, develop jurisdictions, areas of work that those professions consider to be legitimately under their control. The principal goal of most professions is to expand their jurisdictional claims and boundaries, and to achieve what Abbott labels "full and final jurisdiction."[11] The history of the system of professions is a history of jurisdictional claims and disputes, a history of professions constantly expanding by making new jurisdictional claims, protecting themselves from others' claims, and sometimes suffering from weakened claims and hence encroachment by another profession.[12]

But as Abbott points out, every profession encounters problems for which it lacks solutions, "crucial anomalies" that professions often try to deal with through stopgap measures.[13] These anomalies, and the insufficient and temporary means that professions use to cover up their inability to solve these problems, can render a profession vulnerable, whether to the delegitimation of that profession's claims to jurisdiction, or to poaching by other professions that can claim effective treatment for these problems. Crucial anomalies can also render a profession vulnerable in the eyes of the State. While in order to win claims to professional jurisdiction professions tend to abolish all hints of ambiguity, in practice they usually encounter all sorts of uncertainty that needs to be concealed, if not resolved, in the profession's struggle for legitimation.[14]

La question sociale was nineteenth-century political economy's crucial anomaly. For economists, *la question sociale* was a new element of uncertainty thrown up by political economy's encounter with the practical realm of the economy, a changed circumstance that had rendered political economy's jurisdictional claims insecure. By the 1830s and on into the 1840s and 1850s, political economists' writings demonstrate an understanding of their vulnerability to a social problem which the basic tenets of their science suggested ought not to have existed and for which their proposed solution—*laissez-faire*—was looking increasingly ineffectual and unpopular. And certainly the variety of people engaging in discussions of *la question sociale* suggest that political economists would have been justified in worrying about poaching. Not only industrialists, but also a variety of other professionals, politicians of various stripes, the Church, as well as the State itself, were beginning to step onto the terrain that political economists had marked out for themselves.

What means did French political economy have to protect its jurisdiction and to prevent poaching? In 1850 political economy could claim only four academic posts in the French university system: the chair of *économie industrielle* at the *Conservatoire des arts et métiers*; the chair of *histoire et d'économie industrielle* at the *École supérieure de commerce de Paris*; the chair of *économie politique* at the *Collège de France*; and the chair of *économie* at the *École des Ponts et Chaussées*. The paucity of these few posts was underscored by their relative marginality, their exile to the peripheries of the French educational system. For instance, while the chair of political economy at the *Collège de France* enjoyed a long history as one of the anchors of political economy's self-promotion, the *Collège* was unique—it still is—in that it had no real students, gave no examinations, handed out no degrees, prepared no students for particular examinations and precise careers, and had no coherent curriculum.[15] Thus, while they enjoyed the status that came from a chair at this prestigious, albeit unconventional institution, political economists had no means of turning this status into trained economic professionals who could take these ideas out into the mainstream; they had no way of turning this status into acceptance of political economy as a necessary part of degree programs in French higher education; and they had no automatic means of parlaying their post at the *Collège de France* into additional ones.

Similarly, while French political economy had formal organizational structures to assist in the articulation of its claims and to improve its chances of winning jurisdictional disputes, as of 1850 their work was not yet done.[16] The *Journal des économistes* had been conceived by political economists as an academic journal, as well as a means of publicity for their new science, a place from which economists could voice their jurisdictional claims on behalf of political economy to public opinion. Whatever its aspirations, though, the *Journal* was hardly a mainstream journal, and certainly never reached enough readers to constitute a "public." The *Société d'Économie Politique* did unite most French economists, and lobbied on behalf of political economy to the government, but at eighty members in 1850, the *Société* was hardly an army.[17]

Furthermore, the events of 1848, and the suspicion of the republican government toward political economy and the practice of *laissez-faire*, only confirmed the insecurity of French economists. After the Revolution of 1848, both the chairs of political economy at the *Collège de France* and the *École des Ponts et Chaussées* were suppressed.[18] If this were not sufficient warning to political economists of the threat to their science, Lamartine's letter in response to economists' protests, reprinted in the *Journal des économistes*, made the government's position very clear:

> This science [political economy], citizens, must no longer be, as it used to be, the science of wealth. The democratic Republic must and wants to give it another character. It wants to make it the science of brotherhood, the science by which not only labor and its fruits are increased, but by which a more general, fair and universal distribution of wealth among all people will be accomplished. The old science concerned itself only with making individuals richer. The new science will apply itself to making the people as a whole richer.[19]

While both chairs were reinstated after the June Days, Lamartine's warning and the institutional blow that accompanied it could only have suggested to economists the political quicksand upon which their science stood, and the absence of sufficient institutional anchors to help it weather political storms.

By 1850, then, French political economists recognized the precarious position of their science. To achieve their professional ambitions, political economists had presented themselves as scientists, observing and studying natural laws, and operating at all times with a coherent and formal system of knowledge that backed up their pronouncements. This scientific legitimacy, the unified and coherent system of knowledge, the certainty of economists' natural laws: all this is what *la question sociale*, with its countless explanations and possible solutions, had endangered. That their science could no longer propose an exclusively hands-off, *laissez-faire* solution to social misery was demonstrated not only by industrialists practicing paternalism, but by the State which had begun to propose and implement state-administered solutions to particular facets of *la question sociale*.[20] In short, by the mid-nineteenth century economists recognized that everything they had already accomplished might be at risk, and everything they continued to aspire to out of reach. Recognizing the challenge, political economists confronted it. Their solution was to invent a flexible and ambiguous category—usually but not exclusively labeled *économie sociale*—to house the crucial anomaly that was *la question sociale*. Political economists strengthened their discipline not by colonizing new turf, or by making new, more expansive jurisdictional claims, but by segregating out inconvenient data into a separate jurisdiction, the jurisdiction of social economy. To protect the boundaries of their discipline, their jurisdictional claims, and their ambitions as scientists, economists invented a residual category, something that fell outside the narrow confines of political economy yet remained conveniently contiguous, into which could be placed all that uncomfortable information they could not fit seamlessly into their science.

The Physiognomy of Social Economy

Historians seem to agree that the first significant appearance of the term *économie sociale* was in Jean-Baptiste Say's *Cour complet d'économie politique*, published in 1828:

> The study that has been done of nature and the functions of the human body has created a body of ideas, a science which has been given the name of "physiology." The study of the nature and the functions of the social body has also created a science: political economy, or better, social economy [*l'economie politique, ou mieux, sociale*].[21]

Although what Say meant by a "study of the nature and the functions of the social body" would continue to perplex political economists throughout the nineteenth century, their study of the nature and functions of the social body—their efforts to *do* social economy—were remarkably consistent. Possibly the best known piece of "social economic" writing in the nineteenth century was

Louis-René Villermé's *Tableau de l'état physique et moral des ouvriers employés dans les manufactures de coton, de laine, et de soie*, published in 1840. But other prominent economists also contributed to this growing body of literature, and since Villermé is so well-known, I have chosen instead to focus on Louis Reybaud, who wrote an entire series on what he called the *condition morale, matérielle et intellectuelle* of French workers, as representative of social economic thinking among political economists.

On paper, social economy took the form of a) detailed descriptions of working-class living and working conditions; b) intricate and ambiguous explanations of the problems found among workers, with a strong emphasis upon the lack of what economists labeled "morality"; and c) possible solutions to these problems, with a pronounced emphasis upon the strengths of industrial paternalism and the flaws of state-administered solutions. This formula was repeated in all social economic writings, Reybaud's being no exception. Within his analyses of the French cotton, wool, iron, and silk industries were stock descriptions, explanations, and judgments of the social question with which most economists would have agreed.

True to his titles, Reybaud spent considerable time describing the moral, material, and intellectual conditions of workers' lives in industrial regions, focusing on wages, workplace conditions, the quality of homes and home lives, whether or not women and children worked, and what form sociability took. And, as with most social economic tracts, he concluded that industry had improved workers' material conditions but debased their moral conditions. The natural links between workers and their employers, and between family members, had been weakened if not destroyed in industrial regions, leaving workers to vices, foremost among which was alcoholic excess. And although working-class women sometimes tried to combat their husbands' alcoholism by waiting at the doors of factories in order to coax them home, these efforts sometimes had even worse consequences:

> Other [women], unhappy in these first efforts, finish by becoming the accomplices of the excesses against which they tried to fight, and settle down with their husbands or their lovers around pitchers of wine or beer mugs, thereby creating the spectacle of drunkenness in its most degrading form.[22]

Reybaud was uncertain as to the causes of this debased moral condition, an ambiguity characteristic of much social economy. On the one hand, he indicted what he saw to be workers' own vulnerability to immorality: their bad habits, lack of foresight, immorality, and ignorance. Insufficient wages were not the problem, he pointed out. Intelligently-used, they would be sufficient for all workers' needs.[23] But using wages for alcohol, or for the theatre, or for unnecessary luxuries, condemned workers to a life of physical squalor. Workers also exhibited what Reybaud considered to be a foolish and self-defeating obstinacy. He described, for instance, workers in the textile city of Lille who, when evacuated from insalubrious cellar housing, chose to move to equally noxious housing in small, dirty, unsanitary alleys rather than into the newer, healthier neighborhoods constructed for them by industrialists.[24] Or the case of Alsatian workers who preferred to buy their bread at full price in local bakeries rather than at wholesale price at bakeries run by industrialists.[25]

But, Reybaud implied, workers' misery could not be blamed entirely on workers. Greedy employers contributed to this misery, and although by mid-century many had recognized their moral duty to, and responsibility for, their workers, there were still men who "thought more of labor than of men, more of their own interests than of their duties."[26] Such was the case with employers who overlooked their workers' bad habits, thereby undermining the efforts of some employers to eradicate problems of drunkenness, absenteeism, and financial waste. Whereas certain industrialists had begun to pay workers during the week rather than on Saturdays, and to fire workers for habitual absences on Mondays, other industrialists ignored these problems, hiring and keeping workers no matter their habits.[27] Such disregard for workers' well-being, whether material or moral, was, according to Reybaud, inexcusable:

> The reason really stems from the indifference of an industrialist toward anything that does not absolutely affect his business. With regard to discipline in the workshops, he is like iron; breaches of discipline, were they not punished, would cause him losses. He therefore deals severely with them, using fines and expulsions. With regard to outside discipline, he is less rigid, if not downright unconcerned. The worker has completed his task, received his wages; little does it matter if a part [of those wages] is diverted from the family to the cabaret. The industrialist doesn't have to intervene; he believes himself to be completely uninterested.[28]

And finally, Reybaud suggested that the economy itself might have something to do with workers' misery. Although hesitant on this point, he implied that the natural, balanced laws governing the economy did not always work perfectly, and could take time to establish themselves. And in the meantime workers suffered.

Whatever their uncertainty as to the causes of workers' misery, however, Reybaud and others were confident about its solution. Like many industrialists, by the mid-nineteenth century Reybaud had begun to argue that industrial paternalism offered a remedy for the problems of workers. Transcending the impersonal wage contract was an indispensable social link between a manufacturer and a worker:

> One could say...that the employer puts himself in place of the worker, and wants to think, act, calculate for him....In the gorges of the Vosges mountains as on the plains, one will find this vigilant attention given to the condition of man, this paternal sentiment which succeeds through the most ingenious methods of turning him from the bad and conducting him toward the good...[29]

The bulk of Reybaud's work on the "moral, material, and intellectual condition" of French workers was devoted to descriptions of paternalist projects and their results. The aim of his long analyses of working-class housing, health care, education, and retirement and insurance funds was, according to Reybaud, to demonstrate that the benefit of paternalism lay in its emphasis not only on workers' professional lives, but also on their private lives. If the source of workers' problems lay fundamentally outside the factory, then the solution lay fundamentally outside the factory as well. Hence the nature of paternalism: the attention to workers' morality, the attempts to instill certain types of behaviors and to eradicate others, the emphasis upon education, the focus upon the family, the home, private life, and sociability.[30]

Reybaud emphasized the potential economic benefits of paternalist labor management strategies. Paternalism, which created secure, comfortable, and happy working-class families, also ensured economic prosperity, social peace, and political stability. "Workers who have become more sober have become workers who are more reliable, and this moral victory has simultaneously been a good calculation," argued Reybaud.[31] But what about those industrialists who refused to shoulder their moral responsibility? And here Reybaud demonstrated the degree to which mid-century political economists had already diverged from the path of their predecessors. Reluctantly he admitted that "if good will was lacking among our manufacturers, the law ought to stand in for it."[32] But state intervention could only be the last resort, and it could never be as effective a remedy for working-class misery as paternalism.[33] State action simply did not offer what workers really needed:

> There is no deterrent which can replace man's conscience; he can respect nothing when he no longer respects himself. How can we give him back this love of duty and this feeling of personal dignity which are the great safeguards of life? Through education and also through example.[34]

Implicit in this statement was economists' prevailing argument that industrialists, who could provide education and example, held the keys to the solution of *la question sociale.*

What this synopsis of Reybaud's *économie sociale* obscures, however, is the convoluted debates that underlay and accompanied such thinking. The appearance and use of *économie sociale* was never unproblematic or uniform. Instead, *économie sociale* was always accompanied by uncertainty, by debates over what exactly it was, how to properly define and label it, and how to set its boundaries vis-à-vis political economy. Political economists' forays into social economy, their forays into *la question sociale* and its solution, gave rise to deliberations about what it meant to be speaking about discipline, management, and working-class housing, morality, gardens, and retirement funds. Were they, in fact, simply doing political economy as it was meant to be done? Or, if they were doing something other than political economy, what was the relationship between their discussions of prices, wages, supply and demand curves, and international tariffs, and their discussions of misery, paternalism, housing, morality, discipline, and gardens? And what to call this new topic of debate? Was it "political" economy? Was it "new" political economy? Or was it "social" economy?

On first glance, economists' discussions of the proper label for their new discussions of *la question sociale* would appear to be insignificant and arcane definitional issues, obscure exercises in semantics, of interest only to the most committed nineteenth-century political economist. What held these various definitions together, however, and what these discussions reveal, is economists' recognition that political economy as it stood was insufficient to deal with the social and economic problems that French society faced, and hence, that political economy needed to change, to widen, to become more adaptable. Economists' debates over definitions not only demonstrate the manner in which economists tried to graft *la question sociale*, however awkwardly, onto political economy, but also the way they tried to create an addendum, or a new jurisdiction, to hold all those problems relating to working-class misery. Convoluted debates over labels, definitions, and boundaries constituted the process by which economists constructed *économie sociale*, a new category to hold the unexpected *question sociale*.

Not surprisingly, the process of creating the ambiguous and flexible category of *économie sociale* was equally ambiguous, open-ended, and flexible. Economists seldom discussed why, in fact, they cared about the distinctions between "old" and "new" political economy; they certainly did not suggest that what they were doing was creating a category called *économie sociale*. Nor can one locate any moment at which economists achieved agreement on issues of labels, definitions, and boundaries, a point at which one can determine, once and for all, that *économie sociale*, in its finalized form, existed. Nevertheless, through these debates over social economy a lexicon was made available to political economists. An array of vocabulary, a set of basic ideas, and a set of basic judgments and conclusions about *la question sociale* and how it fit into, or next to, political economy, all emerged from these debates over seemingly obscure questions.

As one of the founders of their discipline, Jean-Baptiste Say's definition of political economy was of interest to economists struggling with the implications of *la question sociale*. His definition of political economy in his 1828 *Cour complet d'économie politique*, cited above, suggested that political economy was more than simply a narrow study of wealth; that it was the study of the interaction between various parts of society. Say's wide definition posited no incompatibility between political and social economy; *économie sociale* was simply a better name for political economy, emphasizing its broader concerns. This apparent interchangeability of terms was echoed in Say's efforts on behalf of political economy courses. When discussing possible titles for these courses, Say apparently used *économie politique*, *économie industrielle*, *économie commerciale*, and *économie manufacturière* synonymously, but preferred—as his statement in his 1828 *Cour* makes clear—the term *économie sociale*.[35]

Economists maintained Say's definition of social economy as a general economics of the social body throughout the nineteenth century, although sometimes, but not always, in a slightly different vocabulary. In 1847, for instance, Jean-Baptiste-Firmin Marbeau implied that social economy was a general study of society, branches of which included (1) political economy, the study of how labor leads to happiness and well-being; (2) moral economy, the study of how good behavior leads to happiness and well-being; and (3) charitable economy, the study of how charity, when given intelligently, leads to happiness and well-being.[36]

The interchangeability of the terms *économie politique* and *économie sociale* was maintained throughout his career by economist Joseph Garnier, who argued that social and political economy were essentially the same basic science, with "social economy" simply a better, more comprehensive term than "political economy." But in response to a colleague who argued in favor of replacing the term "political economy" with "social economy" in order to designate the growing interest in *la question sociale*, Garnier argued that political economy had always been concerned with social questions, and that the term *économie sociale* was simply a synonym for *économie politique*: "political or social, they are one; the first is Greek, and the second is Latin, that is all."[37] Garnier's contribution to economists' debates over proper terminology for their science is significant for a variety of reasons. First, it confirms Jean-Baptiste Say's original understanding of the terms and the relationship between *économie politique* and *économie sociale*. Second, it is important as an explicit reference to the appearance of *la question sociale* and to the problem that it posed for political economy. Garnier's statement is a good example of an economist arguing that political economy had *never* been a science uninterested or unconcerned with social questions, that political economy had always been a widely and broadly defined science, one whose label—*économie politique*—inherently implied everything contained within the term *économie sociale*. Third and finally, Garnier's statement suggests the extraordinary disagreement among economists about how to label their science and its new addendum. Garnier, while admitting that *économie sociale* was just a better name for the science that had come to be known as *économie politique*, was nonetheless unwilling to substitute the first term for the second, suggesting either an unwillingness to change old habits, or more probably, the implicit belief that there in fact *was* some difference between *économie sociale* and *économie politique*, and that the two were more useful as separate categories.[38]

An 1859 book review in the *Journal des économistes* offers another case in point. Under review was the *Principes de la science du bien-être social, de l'économie publique et de l'économie des états*, by an Italian economist, Louis Bianchini.[39] In his book, Bianchini severely criticized nineteenth-century political economy in both Britain and France for limiting its scope to an explanation of how to become rich. The significance of political economy in Italy, he argued, was not only that it had tried to conserve the discipline's original eighteenth-century status as a "social science," but that it had tried to expand political economy beyond its original limits, thereby replacing it with a new science of social well-being [*la science du bien-être social*] which combined the accepted principles of political economy with elements of ethics, public law, politics, and administrative science. Calling Bianchini's book a remarkable treatise on *économie sociale*, the French reviewer, A. Leymarie, argued that its real merit was not its attempt to create a new science, but its attempt to restore political economy's real and true character. For Leymarie, Bianchini's new *science du bien-être social*, what Leymarie labeled *économie sociale*, was really just political economy as it had originally been conceived and was supposed to be, that is, a science concerned with more than simply the study of wealth.

Whether explicitly or not, political economists defined social economy and its various synonyms as comprising a concern with the effects of industrialization and the condition of the working class, in other words, with *la question sociale*. This explicit link between *économie sociale* and *la question sociale* was broached at an 1867 meeting of the *Société d'économie politique*, a meeting that also illuminated the extent of economists' disagreement over the proper label for social economy, and the many terms they used to refer to discussions of *la question sociale*.[40] Under discussion was the comparison between "old" and "new" political economy, or as other economists present at that meeting labeled them, "political" and "social" economy, "bourgeois" and "democratic" economy, or "applied" and "pure" political economy. At this meeting, M. Horn argued that in an increasingly democratic society, in which more and more people were turning their attention to the needs and the well-being of the masses, circumstances demanded a widening of the science of political economy, a shift away from its narrow focus on the production of wealth.[41] To signal this new development within political economy, the term *économie politique* should be replaced by *économie sociale*. But not all economists had recognized and understood these new social developments and thus the necessity for political economy to change, and for their inactivity Horn blamed those economists trained in the early nineteenth century:

> They have stayed in the simply negative tendency of *laissez-faire, laissez-passer*, good enough for the classes that have the power to do [*le pouvoir de faire*] and the fortune to get by [*la fortune pour passer*]; they have not paid enough attention to the positive side of the question, to the working classes who must be taught to do, and must be helped to get by.[42]

It was here, in response to Horn's suggestion that "bourgeois" political economy had failed to sufficiently examine *la question sociale*, that Joseph Garnier denied that political economy had ever neglected social questions and pointed out that *économie sociale* was simply a synonym for *économie politique*, one adjective derived from Greek, the other from Latin.[43]

Clearly both men believed that they were in the midst of a profound disagreement: over the history of political economy, over its proper concerns, over its proper label. What matters in this interchange, however, is not their disagreement, but rather the two men's fundamental agreement. Both men were trying to understand what *la question sociale* meant for their science; both men were struggling to make *la question sociale* a legitimate arena of political economic concern. For Horn, "old" political economy had been wrong to neglect social questions; it needed to evolve and thus make these new concerns part of its science. In order to suggest this evolution, this "new" and "democratic" political economy should be renamed social economy. For Garnier, however, "old" political economy had never been uninterested in social questions, had never neglected issues of workers, had never been the narrowly-defined study of wealth, committed inflexibly to the idea of *laissez-faire*, that Horn accused it of being. *La question sociale*, according to Garnier, had *always* fallen within the purview of political economy.

The array of definitions attributed to political and social economy by economists over the course of the nineteenth century provides a glimpse into the sheer flexibility of the category *économie sociale*, which could be fashioned and refashioned depending upon particular requirements or points of view. Social economy could be a general economic science, or a sub-set of political economy, or simply one among many schools of economic thought. It could be a synonym for political economy, or it could replace the term *économie politique* as a better, more comprehensive label. *Économie sociale* could represent political economy as it was originally intended to be, or as it ought to become. When economists spoke of *la question sociale* and offered explanations and/or solutions, it might be social economy they were doing, or it might be "new" political economy, or "democratic" political economy, or "applied" political economy. Rather than any single consistent definition of *économie sociale*, or consistent understanding of what economists were doing when they explored *la question sociale*, there was a morass of definitions, understandings, labels, genealogies. What matters is not which definition of social economy was correct, but rather what this morass meant, how it functioned, and what it did for economists.

These debates also begin to expose the process, treated at greater length below, by which the vague and flexible category of *économie sociale*—with all its synonyms—allowed economists to re-discipline their discipline, creating a space whose definitions and borders were unclear and disputed, but a space which nonetheless could safely house those new topics that had escaped the narrow disciplinary framework of political economy. If wealth could be defined more broadly, then perhaps a concern with working-class happiness, productivity, and morality could be seen as part of a scientific concern with wealth. If political economy were meant to be an adaptable science, then perhaps discussions of *la question sociale* and its paternalist solution were manifestations of that adaptability. And finally, if political economy were originally intended to be a wide social science that studied happiness and well-being alongside wealth, then economists not only could participate authoritatively in discussions of the social question, but continue to pursue their professional ambitions and their efforts to win the institutionalization of their discipline.

One of the challenges of writing as an historian about nineteenth-century social economy is how to grapple with its lack of a firm outline. The variety of terminology used, of people claiming the right to use and define the term *économie sociale,* of institutional loci for its discussion, not to mention its necessarily ambiguous and flexible nature: all this has served to make studying social economy a difficult task.[44] Historians have often mirrored political economists' own confusion over social economy, disagreeing over its definition, origin, and history, and thus shouldering the same burden as economists: to struggle with and solve the problem of social economy. Yet despite their finest efforts, historians have never been able to construct a coherent definition of social economy. To put it bluntly, no one can agree on what *économie sociale* "really" was. To insist on the flexibility of the category of social economy, then, and to refuse to come up with an unequivocal definition other than its residual character, makes it possible to dispense with the inconclusive debate over "what social economy really was" in which first economists, and now historians, have engaged. To argue that social economy represented a broad and malleable spectrum of ideas related to *la question sociale,* that it was nothing more concrete or distinct than a "sensibility,"[45] is to make the indefinability of social economy its most significant and useful feature. Attention to the fundamentally indefinable quality of *économie sociale* allows one, for instance, to examine the debates over the definition and labeling of political and social economy, and dispense with the effort to figure out which definition was *right,* which economist had correctly defined social economy and identified its proper relationship vis-à-vis political economy, and instead to observe all these men using social economy as a means of making *la question sociale* part of the science of political economy. It was social economy's elasticity which allowed political economists to graft *la question sociale* onto their discipline while still protecting it as a scientific discipline resting upon the foundational assumptions of laissez-faire. It was the indefinability of social economy that allowed economists to protect their professional ambitions to see their science given the institutional foundations and status it deserved, and yet nonetheless to contribute to a public debate over social misery that had demonstrated that the economy was far from a universally harmonious space, *laissez-faire* far from the best managerial strategy, and political economy far from a certain science like physics or mathematics.

The "Disciplining" of the Discipline, or the Use of Social Economy

How did the indefinability and thus malleability of *économie sociale* make it possible for political economists to discipline their increasingly unruly discipline? In other words, how exactly did social economy *work*? To answer these questions, I examine one particular debate that preoccupied political economists during the second half of the nineteenth century, a debate over the science and the art of political economy. If some mid-century political economists continued to claim that political economy *was* a science—with a few minor differences from physics and chemistry—others had begun to claim that political economy contained an element of art which distinguished it from the natural sciences, and which compelled it to engage with the lived social consequences of the economic laws and phenomena it observed and explained. Economists' discussions of whether political economy was a science or an art, and what exactly they were doing (science? art? both?) when they discussed *la question sociale* and advocated that industrialists shoulder their responsibility to mitigate it, is one particular place to observe the processes of border patrol and protection that social economy permitted economists. One catches a glimpse of a discipline engaged in disciplining, or managing, the "crucial anomaly" that was *la question sociale*; a glimpse of a discipline rethinking, and thus protecting, its framework, theoretical assumptions, and borders, all of which had been called into question by unanticipated information and new circumstances. This debate demonstrates how economists used *économie sociale* as a place to segregate out inconvenient data, and illustrates the process by which social economy allowed political economists to simultaneously graft *la question sociale* onto their discipline while nonetheless maintaining their scientific claims and aspirations.

Whether political economy constituted an art or a science appears to have been a topic of debate from early in its history. In fact, in the first volume of the *Journal des économistes*, published in 1841, Adolphe Blaise, a regular contributor to the *Journal* and one of the original founding members of the *Société d'économie politique*, took issue with fellow economist Michel Chevalier's characterization of political economy as an art rather than a science. "It is perfectly evident," Blaise wrote:

> that the mission of political economy, and we want to talk about the science here, is not to teach how material interests are organized; because organization is not science, it is art. The organizer must necessarily pay attention to the milieu in which he wants to act; he needs to arrange his terrain in advance, and to prepare the means of transition which must spare the painful strains to the different parts of the body that he is organizing. The scholar does not engage with these details and rejects these temperaments; he confesses the truth as it is, and does not descend into application.[46]

And furthermore:

> When it [political economy] proves the advantages of the most economical production possible, it does as mathematicians do with regard to physics: it supposes a vacuum [*le vide*]. That is to say, that it does not concern itself with knowing whether or not the employment of women in factories entails demoralization and debauchery, or whether or not the employment of children compromises the future recruitment of the army. It is for ethics and politics to observe these facts; they are not of its [political economy's] domain.[47]

Blaise's statement is significant for its defense of political economy as a science similar to mathematics and physics in its amorality, precision, and disinterestedness; women's and children's factory employment and its long-term moral and economic consequences were not the concerns of the science of political economy, he argued most emphatically. But what is also significant about Blaise's article, and suggestive of how economists constantly tried to stretch the boundaries of their science while maintaining its "scientificity," was how Blaise nonetheless tried to create room for *la question sociale*, even after having dismissed it. He went on to describe three levels of political economic thought: pure political economy, which offered abstract and generalized truth on the subject of the economy; applied political economy, which offered modified truths based upon circumstances of time or place; and government, which he defined as the union of both pure and applied political economy with morality and politics. The work of Michel Chevalier, the explicit target of Blaise's critiques, was placed in the third, and in Blaise's mind, most definitely inferior, category. The category of applied political economy, however, was associated with Jerome-Adolphe Blanqui's courses at the *Conservatoire des Arts et Métiers,* and while Blaise clearly ranked applied political economy below pure political economy, the category of application did not receive the same type of deprecation as government.[48]

So what was this category of applied political economy? What exactly did it comprise? These are the questions that Blaise left unanswered, and these are the questions that other political economists would continue to ask, and continue to leave unanswered, throughout the century. But certainly this category opened up a place for engagement with social problems, a place all of political economy's own, outside what Blaise termed "government." In the same year that Blaise categorized these different political economies, Jerome-Adolphe Blanqui had emphatically pointed to the disastrous social consequences of *laissez-faire.* 1841 was the same year that Louis Reybaud admitted that political economy and its supposedly universal and harmonious laws had not been able to solve the problems suffered by France's working population. Examining Blaise's category of applied political economy in this context, then, suggests that this was a space–while not named social economy–that could hold *la question sociale* without endangering the science of pure political economy. Political economy might be a science, in Blaise's mind, but the creation of a space outside that science could nonetheless allow economists to engage with *la question sociale,* and to legitimately graft questions like the long-term consequences of women's and children's factory labor onto their science.

In 1851, Charles Coquelin, editor of the *Dictionnaire de l'économie politique* and author of its entry on political economy, offered general definitions of "art" and "science":

> An art consists of a series of precepts or rules to follow, a science of the understanding of certain phenomena, or certain observed and revealed connections....An art advises, prescribes, directs, a science observes, exposes, and explains....Thus, to observe and describe real phenomena, that is science; to dictate precepts, prescribe rules, that is art.[49]

Consistent with this original definition, the *Nouveau dictionnaire d'économie politique,* written forty years later, defined a science as the study of natural, permanent, and universal phenomena. In contrast, an art was the product of human actions and decisions; it studied temporary, variable, and human phenomena.[50] Hence, whereas a science remained constant and universally valid, an art naturally evolved. But as Ambroise Clément pointed out in his introductory essay to the *Dictionnaire*, the constancy of science did not necessarily mean homogeneity of opinions among scientists. There were no sciences, he wrote, not even the science of pure mathematics, which had not experienced differing opinions on the facts that those sciences purported to observe, study, and explain. Differences of opinion, then, were perfectly compatible with scientific status; disagreement and debate were normal components of any science.[51] An art, furthermore, studied existing conditions with an eye toward improving them. As economist Courcelle-Seneuil argued in 1878, the object of an art was to serve human needs.[52] For political economists, art entailed application. They argued that identical solutions were seldom appropriate for the problems of different cultures, regions, nations or eras. It was the goal of any applied science to distinguish alternate solutions or ways of applying scientific principles to a single problem.

What, then, was political economy? According to the editor of the *Dictionnaire de l'économie politique*, political economy was both a science and an art because it encompassed explanations of natural economic phenomena as well as advice, precepts, and rules.[53] Although Adam Smith had defined political economy more as an art and Jean-Baptiste Say more as a science, both were correct. Political economy was simultaneously the study of human industry, and the study of wealth and its increase on behalf of all people. The science of political economy studied how human beings exerted themselves, while the art of political economy studied the results of those efforts.

By mid-century, this notion of political economy as both a science and an art had become a constant theme among most economists. And by the time the *Nouveau dictionnaire d'économie politique* was published in 1891, the art of political economy had been defined as encompassing the effects of industrialization and the search for possible solutions:

> Applied political economy is an art which has for a long time been limited to the search for the conditions by which a people can become as rich as possible. Today, this goal is mingling with the goal of the social art [*l'art social*]: to search for the conditions by which society can keep alive the greatest number of people in the best possible conditions.[54]

The relationship between the science and art of political economy was a complementary one, economists argued. Without each other, both were diminished:

> It is not good that scientific truths remain sterile, and the only manner of using them is to deduce an art from them. There are, as we have already said, tight links of kinship between the science and the art. Science lends to art its knowledge, it rectifies its procedures, it enlightens and directs its course. Without the help of science, art can advance only gropingly, stumbling at every step. On the other hand, it is art which highlights the truths that science has discovered, and without which science would remain sterile.[55]

No longer was the goal of the science of political economy to remain aloof from daily life and from the consequences of the economic laws and phenomena it observed, described, and explained. Instead, "a science is destined to serve: it is an exercise with a view to action and struggle."[56] In a telling critique of some of the (unnamed) economists who had followed Adam Smith, economist Hippolyte Passy accused them of wanting to turn political economy into a mathematical science, devoid of human beings and immune to real social conditions:

> Uniquely preoccupied with wealth realized in its material form, forgetting that man is simultaneously its author and its end, that it is man who creates wealth, uses it and consumes it, they took no account of the conditions that are needed for the success of his [man's] efforts; and if they had been alone at work, political economy would have become a sort of mathematical science, dealing with fixed element, numerical quantities, and forces with an invariable intensity.[57]

Participants in these discussions were careful, however, to always maintain a proper hierarchy between the science and art of political economy, always describing the art as subordinate to the science. Although the art of political economy took into account circumstances, and hence could not always apply political economic theory completely and universally, it was to be derived as closely as possible from the science of political economy, which ranked much higher in significance and authority:

> Science and art are things simultaneously distinct and closely related. Discovering and proclaiming general truths is the mission of science; realizing these truths in practice the mission of art....But in this work art remains the agent and the servant of science. It is [science] that indicates the goal to attain, the principals and the truths whose triumph must be prepared....[58]

That this category of art or applied political economy was an awkward one, poorly-defined and amorphous, did not go unnoticed. In a January 1864 meeting of the *Société d'économie politique*, one member pointed out that the imprecision of the distinction between pure and applied political economy had left members of the public with the impression that political economy was a conjectural, rather than an exact science, that it had more in common with medicine, with its variable features, than with anatomy and physiology with their invariable and certain features.[59] These worries may have been realistic ones; given that the amorphousness of applied political economy sometimes puzzled political economists themselves, it can only have confused outsiders. And yet the continued efforts to use categories like applied political economy, or social economy, or the art of political economy, suggested that the advantages of an amorphous category offset the disadvantages of possibly complicating and muddling their science. It gave economists a place to house unpleasant information that they could not deny; to claim that political economy really did pay attention to real people and real social conditions; to assert that it was a relevant science, even a moral science. Whereas their definitions of a moral science were as imprecise and elusive as their definitions of social economy, by the mid-nineteenth century a growing number of economists were nonetheless arguing that political economy shared certain traits with the moral sciences of ethics, law and politics.[60] By the mid-nineteenth century the idea of political economy as an *amoral* science had become increasingly unpleasant to many economists; in the face of proven social misery, and in the face of efforts to solve that misery (many of those efforts by the same state that distributed academic positions), *amoral* seemed to come uncomfortably close to *immoral*.

What the member of the *Sociéte d'économie politique*, worried about the amorphousness of art, seems to have noticed is that the effort to graft *la question sociale* onto political economy was an awkward proposition, difficult to accomplish successfully and without repercussions. And yet it was the effort to graft unanticipated information onto a science, not the success of the graft, which is significant. The fuzziness, flexibility, or inexactitude of applied political economy, or the art of political economy, or social economy, were precisely the qualities that allowed it to house the wide array of topics that political economy both claimed and refused, and to remain both *outside* the pure science of political economy, but close enough to make those topics legitimately part of the work of political economy.

In their attempt to wrestle with the relationship between the science and art of political economy, or between pure and applied political economy, certain economists began to rewrite the history of the discipline as a way of legitimizing their new concern with *la question sociale* and paternalism. French economists began to ask themselves whether political economy had originally been defined as a narrow, wealth-based science or as a broadly-based moral science, what the founders of the discipline had intended, and where, when, and how the science had stepped off-track, if that was indeed what had happened. If historians have recently drawn attention to the fallacy of regarding Smith as committed wholeheartedly to *laissez-faire*, and Say as indifferent to social concerns, French economists of the mid-nineteenth century had not yet come to these same conclusions. Discussions within economic circles thus revolved around the issue of what Adam Smith and his followers, Jean-Baptiste Say in particular, had intended political economy to be. For economists, the relationship between Smith and Say and their respective conceptions of political economy, and between what economists increasingly referred to as the English and French schools of political economists, was never unambiguous. In a meeting of the *Société d'économie politique* in 1854, economists tried to define what comprised these two schools:

> There are notably two distinct schools: one which is inspired most particularly by the idea of justice, and another which is inspired most particularly by the idea of utility. It is the English school that is most certainly the school that draws its convictions by preference from utility and convenience, and that shows itself to be more indecisive on ethical principles. This is the school of Malthus, of Ricardo, of MacCulloch, etc., whose sympathies are less generous, less elevated, less humanitarian than those of the economists of the French school...[M. Baudrillart] finds in Adam Smith a broadness of views that draws him closer to the French school, and it must be noted that Smith was not English, but Scottish.[61]

That Adam Smith had, in fact, understood political economy as an art; that he was *not* a member of the English school of political economy; and thus that political economy had become a narrowly-defined and inflexible science of wealth somewhere between the publication of *The Wealth of Nations* in 1776 and Say's *Traité d'économie politique* in 1803: this appears to have been a consensus developing among French economists by mid-century. Between Smith and Say, political economy had stepped off track, and it was thus the duty of political economy to recover what had been lost: the humanitarian perspective, the broad concerns, the art.[62] In his entry on political economy in the *Nouveau dictionnaire d'économie politique*, for instance, economist Courcelle-Seneuil argued that the science of political economy had emerged from the art of political economy. Men had observed economic conditions and phenomena, collected data, formed conclusions, and finally, recognized a pattern of natural laws. A science was thus born. Limiting the scope of this new science to the study of wealth was Adam Smith's essential contribution. This did not mean, however, that Smith had intended to dispense with issues of application or art. For Smith, political economy was still an art that offered precepts designed for application to the real world.

It was this attention to both science and art, to application and theory, that earned the eighteenth century the label "the Golden Age of political economy." But during the nineteenth century, political economy had renounced its links to art and application. It was, Courcelle-Seneuil argued, Jean-Baptiste Say and his followers who abandoned the concern with application, and who began to describe political economy as a science offering analysis rather than advice. The result was that political economy had become a theoretical and abstract study of wealth, not the first time such a charge had been leveled at Say.[63] On a brighter note, however, Courcelle-Seneuil pointed out that late nineteenth-century political economy was engaged in a process of change and correction, that economists were returning to political economy's original breadth and depth, abandoning its temporary and unnatural narrowness in favor of the older definition of political economy which encompassed the entire spectrum of social concerns.[64]

Despite all this rumination on art and science, political economists never explicitly equated the art of political economy, or applied political economy, with the term *économie sociale*. No convenient "smoking gun" exists that clearly and precisely links economists' concerns with art, application, advice, and assistance to the amorphous category labeled *économie sociale*. What *is* unmistakable, however, is the affinity between what economists discussed under the rubric of the "the art of political economy," or "applied political economy," and what they discussed under the rubric of "social economy." The term *économie sociale* was but one label used by economists to refer to a sensibility toward the social consequences of industrialization, toward the consequences of *la question sociale*. Economists' definition of the art of political economy as the study of variable and human phenomena, its method advice and prescription, and its purpose the application of general truths in order to ameliorate social conditions, coincided with discussions of the unforeseen consequences of industrialization, the recognition of and growing fear of what a *laissez-faire* society might threaten, and an advocacy of paternalist labor management. Working out the relationship between the science and the art of political economy, or between political economy and social economy, or between pure and applied political economy, was thus akin to working out the relationship between the original framework of political economy and the new problems that had cast doubt on that framework.

By now it should be apparent that any attempt to precisely define *économie sociale* once and for all is an exercise in futility. This chapter's elucidation of the controversy surrounding social economy—whether it was a science or an art, a continuation of classical economic theory or a violation thereof, an independent subject or one dependent on political economy; whether it should be labeled social economy, the art of political economy, applied political economy, or democratic political economy—suggests the impossibility of devising a single definition for a term about which political economists themselves disagreed, a term whose scope, limits, and content changed regularly. In fact, the only constant definition that can be offered of social economy is that it represented those issues, concerns, and problems—the detritus—that seeped through the conceptual barriers political economists had tried to erect. Social economy was both a residual and a receptacle, something that could not be squeezed into the theoretical framework and assumptions of political economy without damaging them, something that was left over or left outside the parameters of the discipline, as well as the place to store all that anomalous, ill-fitting, and threatening information.

No matter nineteenth-century political economists' efforts to compare their discipline to physics and mathematics, it seems quite obvious that political economy was not—and still is not—comparable to either. Thus the crucial plot twist in the story of nineteenth-century political economy was economists' reluctant realization that however much they aspired to the scientific status achieved by the "hard" sciences, theirs was not *quite* the same type of science. While political economists would have agreed with Foucault that the physical and the human sciences were profoundly different, they would have disagreed vehemently with any classification of political economy among the dubious, or "muddled" sciences.[65] What is interesting about nineteenth-century political economy is its effort to protect its self-definition as a science, its apparent refusal to give up its aspirations to non-dubious scientificity.

One of the characteristics of the social sciences is that they are plagued by anomalies, things that do not work. By the mid-nineteenth century, political economy's gaze upon workers, a gaze that had generated power, had also unfortunately generated unexpected and anomalous knowledge that did not fit political economy's scientific framework and thus threatened the interpretive and prescriptive power economists claimed for themselves. Nineteenth-century French political economists found themselves face to face with a "social question" that suggested that their theories did not work in practice the way they were supposed to. This anomaly gave rise to constant efforts to figure out what this anomaly meant for the science of political economy and its professional ambitions. It forced shifts within political economy in order to protect its claims to legitimately observe its subjects, create knowledge, and then interpret and implement that knowledge. *La question sociale* forced political economists to do on behalf of their discipline something akin to what French industrialists were doing on behalf of their workers: to discipline it, to intervene within it rather than leave it alone, and to rethink their discipline in such a way that the unwanted knowledge could be made part of it.

If *la question sociale* was the anomaly thrown up by political economy, threatening to swamp it, *économie sociale* was constructed by economists as the place to deposit that anomaly, as the bulwark against everything that threatened to expose the dubiousness of their science. It was social economy that allowed political economists to "discipline" their discipline, to corral the unruly, unexpected, and unwanted elements that threatened to undermine their authority and their claims to universal, natural knowledge. Social economy was political economy's complement–external to, hierarchically inferior to, yet still associated with, political economy–into which all those problematic issues associated with industrialization could be placed. This complementarity implied that if the proper function of social economy was the management of human subjects, the proper function of political economy could remain the observation and study of natural laws. The bulwark of social economy made it possible for economists to continue to define political economy as an objective and exact science employing observation and logic, to restrict its area of expertise to the economy and the production of wealth, and to sustain its basic assumptions about laissez-faire, the harmony of social interests, and individual self-determination.

4. The Productive Failures of Political Economy

On September 17, 1864, a government decree created a provisional chair of political economy and public law at the Faculty of Law in Paris. Almost thirteen years later, on March 26, 1877, another decree made that provisional chair permanent, and political economy a required part of the curriculum in every French law faculty. Political economy and political economists could now enjoy the status attendant on a discipline institutionalized as a compulsory subject in France's law schools, schools that surpassed all others in France in the numbers of students served, the prestige attached to their degrees, and the influential professional trajectories of their graduates. Political economists, it would seem, had finally achieved the victory for which they had so assiduously worked: political economy had been thrust from the fringes of academia into the heart of French higher education.[1] And yet that victory was achieved at a cost: the loss of political economy's disciplinary independence; the loss of vigor within political economy's traditional strongholds; the historicization of the heretofore self-declared timeless science of political economy; and the superseding of many of the discipline's foundational tenets. Rather than the 1877 decree signaling the victory of economists' efforts to see political economy institutionalized as a natural, universal, objective, and concrete science, the decree seems instead to have signaled how much political economy had changed from that earlier formulation. Social economy, created to cordon off the dangerous, potentially unscientific, or dubious, parts of the economic discipline, had subtly changed political economy, escaping and proliferating beyond economists' ability to control it. The political economy that finally achieved institutional victory at the *Facultés de Droit* was not the certain and exact "hard" science that economists had been protecting and promoting for decades, but rather a more dubious human science.

Though political economists had invented *économie sociale* as a bulwark against all the dysfunctions of capitalism implied by "the social question," and against the ensuing need for the government of the population and the regulation of industrial capitalism, by the end of the nineteenth century they had lost control of those fortifications. Social economy had spread not only within the borders of political economy, but also beyond them, beyond the ability of political economists to control the meaning and use of the term. The invention of *économie sociale*, that category that could hold all the unexpected and unwanted information thrown up by *la question sociale*, may have helped political economy achieve institutionalization, but in the process it also altered the discipline that economists were scrambling to protect. *Économie sociale* helped launch into public discussion a way of thinking and talking about *la question sociale*—a discourse—that was by its very nature critical of political economy and undermined its basic "scientific" tenets, and that others used for very different purposes and with different consequences than political economists had originally intended. The discourse of *économie sociale* provided the evidence that political economy's grasp of the workings of the economy was, and could only ever be, partial; and suggested not only that *laissez-faire* was not working in practice, but that government, the bane of political economists, might in fact be socially indispensable. In the long run, the apparent intractability of *la question sociale*, the failure of political economy to protect its borders and to fully exclude from its purview all things "social," and thus the dramatic proliferation of the discourse of social economy outside the margins of political economy, have all proven extraordinarily productive. The "social"—the detritus that political economists had relegated to *économie sociale*—has proven itself to be far more socially productive, far more useful, than the discipline of political economy itself and its scientific aspirations. Thus, this chapter will subtly shift away from the history of political economy and its institutional aspirations, to what is in fact much more historically significant; it will shift away from political economy and *its* history, to its failures and *their* histories.

This chapter will narrate French political economy's connection to two "productive failures." The paradoxical nature of the phrase immediately identifies it as Foucauldian in inspiration: how can something unsuccessful nonetheless be productive? According to Michel Foucault, failures are commonly useful, even if what they produce is unintended. For Foucault, the best example of a productive failure is, of course, the failure of prisons to reform criminals, and his *Discipline and Punish* was an analysis of what prisons *do* accomplish, given that they do not turn criminals into law-abiding citizens capable of integrating easily and happily back into conventional social practices.[2] But nineteenth-century French political economy offers a similarly effective vantage point from which to investigate what a productive failure is and how it works, in short, what makes it productive. The first of the productive failures examined in this chapter is political economists' futile effort to protect their science by inventing a category in which to sequester threatening information, a category that eventually escaped their control and launched itself into public discourse as a form of knowledge that legitimated regulatory governmental practices and confirmed expertise upon an array of human scientists working on behalf of the welfare of the population. The second, and more significant, productive failure was the failure—on the part of *everyone*, including political economists—to solve *la question sociale* despite almost a century of efforts, a failure that produced an explosion of information that rendered French workers more visible, better-known, and thus more efficiently governable. What links these two productive failures is, in fact, not just political economy, but industrial capitalism itself. Behind the century-long debate over *la question sociale*; behind political economists' invention of *économie sociale* and their inability to keep that category in check; behind the escape of social economy and its adoption and use by a variety of agents, lay the problem of managing the unanticipated consequences of industrial capitalism. Proponents of industrial capitalism have had, from its inception, to confront its shortcomings. During the nineteenth century, *la question sociale* and social economy anchored the shortcomings of industrial capitalism *outside* of capitalism, *outside* of the economy, in the realm of behavior rather than structure. The story of nineteenth-century French political economy is thus the story of economists' unsuccessful effort to hide the disastrous social consequences of capitalism, to move the dysfunctions of capitalism out of the discipline of economics into other realms, and to protect the science of political economy from the truth of the industrial capitalist economy.

Economists' unsuccessful effort to hide the disastrous social consequences of capitalism, and the successful and productive proliferation of everything economists tried to hide—*la question sociale*—again connects political economy to a topic first addressed in Chapter Two: governmentality, what Michel Foucault described as the network of extra-state administered strategies and programs designed to collect information about both populations and individuals in order to better manage, control and reconfigure them. The boundary that French political economy drew between all things economic and all things social, and its loss of control over the social, was the foundation for governmentality, for the indirect and twisted process toward a mode of modern government whose primary aim was the cultivation of human resources, and the assurance of the health, dependability and productivity of the population. What did the creation and then the proliferation of social economy—with or without control by political economists—make possible, what or who did it make visible, and with what effect? Who or what came to be governed as a result of the creation and proliferation of social economy, that fluid space once created to hold *la question sociale*, and by whom? What opportunities were created to more closely observe, describe, study, assist, normalize, and regulate the French working class by the apparent failure to solve the social question? These are questions that point to the profoundly productive social utility of *la question sociale* and social economy. More precisely, they point to the usefulness of the *failure* to solve *la question sociale*, and thus the proliferation of social economy into wide swaths of the academy, into all of the human sciences, deep into public discourse, and with that proliferation, the spread of regulatory, disciplinary, normalizing power.

The Proliferation of Social Economy

Since 1818, when Jean-Baptiste Say wrote a letter to the Baron Thénard of the *Académie des sciences*, advocating on behalf of a chair of political economy at the *Conservatoire des arts et métiers*[3], political economists had promoted their science as one that contributed to the overall health of the nation by influencing government policy, teaching manufacturers the natural workings of the economy, and encouraging sane and healthy notions among the working classes. It was the belief that theirs was a properly *social* science, a science that contributed to the health and wealth of society, that motivated all of economists' public relations strategies. By 1860, the *Journal des économistes* had begun to demand that the government establish chairs of political economy in the *Facultés de Droit*.[4] As a discipline that analyzed the laws by which the economy, and by extension, society operated, political economy needed to be part of the professional training of the men in charge of overseeing those laws. And in 1864, economists' arguments seemed to have worked. On September 17, 1864, the Minister Victor Duruy created a provisional chair of political economy and public law at the *Faculté de Droit de Paris*.[5] Explaining his decree, Duruy pointed out that political economy was a "complete science," that it was taught everywhere around the world, and that everywhere it was taught it had helped prevent social crises.[6] And because of the number of students graduated by the *Faculté de Droit de Paris*, as well as the high-ranking positions that most of those graduates would come to hold, a chair of political economy was best placed in the law faculty rather than at the Sorbonne.[7] According to historian Lucette Le Van-Lemesle, what finally won political economy the regularization of its chair at the Paris law faculty in 1877, and its inclusion as a required part of the French law curriculum, was economists' success at painting their discipline as one that promoted and taught political stability, as a moderate science—rather than a revolutionary and utopian science—that respected, and taught others to respect, the social order and the right of property.[8] It was this conservative depiction that meant that second-year law students would now be examined in political economy, effectively guaranteeing the discipline, heretofore optional, a compulsory status, and the new chairs of political economy a motivated audience.

Once political economy was institutionalized in the *Facultés de Droit* in 1877, the schools that had previously sheltered it and that had served as important sites of self-promotion, began to fade in importance.[9] Political economy's durable victory in the law faculties was suggested by the declining relevance of the chairs of political economy at the *Collège de France*, at the *Conservatoire des arts et métiers*, at the *École libre des Sciences Politiques.* Economists had always complained of the peripheral nature of these chairs, and once they had achieved victory within the heart of French higher education, the periphery lost most of its vigor. The *Journal des économistes* continued to be published, of course, but it was now joined by competing journals such as *L'économiste français* and the *Revue d'économie politique.* The *Société d'économie politique* continued to meet, and economists continued to be named to the *Académie des sciences morales et politiques.* But the institutionalization of political economy in the law faculties removed the central purpose of these institutions: the task of lobbying on behalf of a suspect science. The consequence of the French state's acknowledgement of political economy's jurisdictional claims in 1877 was that the dynamism of political economy shifted from a network of interlocking institutions to a single institution.

If political economists had tried to protect their discipline from challenges to its scientific coherence by creating *économie sociale* as a *cordon sanitaire*, had this strategy worked? Perhaps. Political economy may have succeeded in 1877 because it had *not* succumbed to an entire rethinking of itself. Instead, its dangerous elements, the elements that were "unscientific" or dubious, the elements that suggested the need for rethinking, had all been relegated elsewhere. Political economy had not abandoned its belief that it was a science: that its job was to observe the economy; that based upon those observations it could offer solutions to economic problems on behalf of the state; that it was neither utopian nor opposed to the *status quo.* Thus, because political economy was still a science, because it still taught how the mechanisms of society worked, rather than how they *should* work, political economists could, and did, argue that economics needed to be part of the curriculum in law schools.

But even as economists tried to use social economy as a means of protecting their own discipline, ultimately they failed to manage the inconsistencies between political economy and *économie sociale*. After 1877 economists had to face the gloomy realization that despite *économie sociale*, their "science" *had* changed; that it had been challenged; that political economy was no longer the same type of science it was in 1830; and that economists had not managed to protect their discipline from becoming dubious. Although political economists had by mid-century started to question the incontrovertibility of *laissez-faire*, political economy's victory in 1877 marked the final blow to the presumed certainty of this principle. According to heterodox economist Charles Gide, writing in 1890, the lawyers who dominated the faculty at the *Facultés de Droit*, even those teaching political economy, were considerably less suspicious of government activity than were economists.[10] In the struggle between justice and wealth (to borrow from the title of Lucette Le Van-Lemesle's book, *Le Juste ou le Riche*), and more precisely, between justice and the unfettered liberty to pursue wealth, the *Facultés de Droit* tended to come down on the side of justice, and thus by extension, on the side of government. In 1873, while the chair of political economy at the *Faculté de Droit de Paris* was still in its provisional stage, Paul-Émile Cauwès, a recent graduate of the *Faculté*, was named to teach the course in political economy. And while that course ostensibly focused upon economic legislation, it also questioned many of the key tenets upon which the science of political economy had theretofore rested.[11] Cauwès was, first of all, a protectionist, arguing that state intervention was indispensable in matters of trade. Furthermore, he believed in social legislation as a means of alleviating the misery of workers and of easing social conflict.[12] While Cauwès accepted some of the premises of orthodox political economy—he believed that free enterprise, for instance, was the most efficient means of producing wealth—there were others he disputed, most significantly the idea of the naturally self-regulating labor market.[13] And it was here that state intervention was necessary, in the form of protectionist tariffs and social legislation, in order to reestablish the equilibrium that "natural laws"—if they existed at all—had failed to do.

While many political economists reacted with horror at what they regarded as a betrayal of their science, this was nonetheless a pattern that would continue at the French law faculties. The political economy taught at the *Facultés de Droit* was far from the certain, natural, harmonious science regulated by universal self-balancing laws to which nineteenth-century economists had been so loyally attached. That the discipline of political economy was no longer a unified one, that institutionalization had created a rift among men who called themselves economists, is suggested by the creation, in 1887, of the *Revue d'économie politique*, an economic journal to rival the *Journal des économistes.* Charles Gide, one of its founders and editors, explained the *Revue* as the result of the monopoly exercised by orthodox economists—Gide refers to them as the "optimistic school," or less flatteringly, as "complacently optimistic"[14]—over economic thought. According to Gide, until the founding of the *Revue d'économie politique*, there had been no public forum in which to present ideas that diverged from conventional economic beliefs. The monopoly exerted by orthodox economists in the *Société d'économie politique*, in the *Académie des sciences morales et politiques*, and in the pages of the *Journal des économistes*, had effectively silenced innovation, and had created the false image of an economic science that had changed little in 50 years.[15]

Gide's introductory essay to the first volume of the *Revue d'économie politique* points not only to philosophic ruptures among economists, but, more importantly, to what political economy had become at the *Facultés de droit.* According to Gide in his 1887 essay, before 1870 political economy appeared to be a "clearly defined, and even perfect science":

> Not only during this time was political economy a science, it was a force. It did not simply teach; it governed. It had more than just disciples; it had courtesans.[16]

But if political economy *had* once been a force, the economic laws upon which the science had based its authority had not proven as certain as economists had always claimed:

> It must be admitted that the laws or hypotheses of the old political economy have given almost everything that they can give. They are now dried up and empty like a lemon that has been squeezed to the rind, precisely because they have not been replenished by the observation of facts.[17]

And it was to this observation of facts that the contributors to the *Revue d'économie politique*, and by extension, professors at the *Facultés de droit*, were committed:

> A good number of economists have thought that henceforth it would be necessary to prohibit all research into so-called economic laws, and that it would be acceptable to limit themselves to a more modest, but more certain task: to study diverse institutions in their historical development...[18]

As it was taught at French law faculties, the discipline of political economy had begun to embrace history, and to become more comfortable with the idea of change over time, and less comfortable with the fundamental assumption of orthodox economists that there were universal, fixed economic laws. Not only did historicization call into question the idea that there were principles that held for all times and all places, but for professors at the *Facultés de Droit*, history had revealed that the "laws" of supply and demand operating during the nineteenth century had not worked, particularly with regard to labor, and that free trade and free competition had actually led to injustices.[19] To embrace history meant a fundamental change in the very nature of the science that was political economy, something that economist Jean-Gustave Courcelle-Seneuil recognized in an 1877 *Journal des économistes* article attacking the political economy taught by Paul-Émile Cauwès at the *Faculté de Droit de Paris*. According to Courcelle-Seneuil, history meant description rather than analysis. It dealt in case studies, which were insufficient as a means of uncovering universal laws.[20] Furthermore, to use history meant breaking with the disdain always displayed by Jean-Baptiste Say, for whom history was a catalog of depressing and sad facts from which it was impossible to infer laws.

Thus, for political economy to turn toward history was to turn from ahistorical universals, from the idea of certainty, and from the idea of political economy as a science akin to physics. History meant the careful attention to historical, social, and cultural context; history meant attention to change over time; history meant the rejection of the idea of universality itself. Just as significantly, history meant that one could start thinking about how circumstances *might* be. If circumstances had once been different than they were now—historical and contingent rather than natural and unchanging—then why could they not be different than they were today? And perhaps one of the tasks of political economy was to hypothesize about how circumstances *could* be better, and then advise as to how to achieve those dreams. According to Charles Gide:

> When one believes that social institutions are in a constant state of "becoming," one is naturally led to ask oneself what they might become, and to think how they might be modified and to research in what way it might be suitable to guide them.[21]

The form that political economy took in French law faculties, and the representation of the economic science by Charles Gide, suggest that despite orthodox economists' efforts to maintain political economy as a certain and scientific discipline by protecting it from the uncertainties and ambiguities of what they called art, the rigid science/art dichotomy they had traditionally employed was beginning to break down, with the certain and universal science of political economy slipping toward an uncertain and ambiguous art. By the 1870s and 1880s, the understanding of science that French economists had inherited–science as defined by universal laws, general patterns, natural and permanent phenomena–was looking increasingly outdated. If Gide's representation of political economy in 1887 is any indication, science now appeared to be compatible with historical change, with a move away from universals toward empiricism, with a shift away from general patterns toward case studies that hinted at unpredictability rather than inevitability. Political economy's transformations at the *Facultés de Droit* moved the discipline away from the physical sciences, and toward something usually called the human sciences, which operated with different techniques and assumptions than the physical sciences.[22] Even as economists, once anxious to protect their science from art, had set up *économie sociale* as a *cordon sanitaire* around political economy, so did they themselves–by engaging in the fact-finding investigations of social economy all the while declaring its inferiority to political economy–chip away at the boundaries between the science of political economy and the art of social economy. As economists hung on to their universals, to their (perhaps outmoded) definitions of what a science was, they also participated in the empirical observations of working-class life that was *économie sociale*, thus breaking down the barriers between the two. Whether or not they recognized it, economists had already lost control of the boundaries of their discipline, a loss of control only made clear to them once political economy had been institutionalized at the *Facultés de Droit* in a form most of them no longer recognized as scientific.

That political economists had already transformed the nature of their science by the 1870s without altogether realizing it is suggested by an exchange of opinions between Jean-Gustave Courcelle-Seneuil and an anonymous critic of the 1877 decree that made political economy a required part of the law curriculum.[23] According to this critic, political economy was not a positive science; at best it was a conjectural art, but it was *certainly* not a branch of the law. More significantly, it was a discipline without precision and without uniformity, a discipline that was understood and taught in a variety of ways.

Lacking uniformity, political economy could not be codified, and lacking codification, political economy lacked rigor. By science, then, this anonymous critic clearly meant a body of knowledge that was exact, that operated according to uniform formulae, and that, as an exact and uniform body of knowledge, could be codified into a single interpretation. This anonymous critic was thus operating according to notions of science that many economists, particularly those writing in the early nineteenth century, would have understood, and would have claimed for political economy.

But in 1877, even to economists who had spent their careers defending the purported science of political economy, the definition of science employed by this critic looked out-of-date. Faced with this definition of science, economist Courcelle-Seneuil made an argument that, while ostensibly protecting the "scientific" nature of political economy from this anonymous attacker, in fact described and defended political economy in terms that marked it as a human science. Courcelle-Seneuil argued that political economy was both a science and an art, that political economy had a scientific nucleus of universal laws that transcended historical and cultural context, but that the economic science also had to contend with that same historical and cultural context, which in fact *did* change. Central to the science of political economy was not simply the observation and codification of the universal laws of the economy, but the analysis of the social consequences of those laws at particular times and places. *How* those universal laws operated in different historical and cultural contexts was the question that the art of political economy took up.

For Courcelle-Seneuil, himself trained in the law, both political economy and the law rested upon general principles, principles which, in the case of political economy, were firmly scientific. Once educated in those general principles, the goal—of an economist, a jurist, or a legislator—was to use that general knowledge to understand, interpret, illuminate, and resolve particular issues which changed from one historical moment to the next. Political economy was both more scientific than the law as it had traditional been understood in France, and more committed to the study of empirical situations. It was both *more* of a science, and more of an art. As Courcelle-Seneuil would go on to say in his essay on political economy in the 1891 *Nouveau dictionnaire d'économie politique*, "a science is destined to serve; it is an exercise with a view to action and struggle."[24] Against his anonymous opponent in 1877, then, Courcelle-Seneuil defended what one might call a more "human" political economy, a more socially-conscious economic science, an economic science that was no less scientific for its acceptance of art, and for its flexibility in the application of general principles to the social realm.[25]

If *la question sociale* had once shaken economists' confidence in the purportedly universal tenets of their certain science, and provoked struggles against disciplinary transformations, 1877 suggests that political economy *had* transformed, that it had–perhaps unbeknownst to economists themselves and despite their efforts to contain, if not prevent, those transformations–shifted away from a presumed resemblance to physics toward a less certain and more human science. By 1877, and certainly by the founding of the *Revue d'économie politique* in 1887, political economy had transformed into a discipline compatible with the law. By its very nature, the law tipped toward the particulars and away from universals, toward the practical and the regulatory, and thus toward policy, public service, and planning. The law tipped toward an emphasis upon justice and toward what political economists referred to as "art." Thus, it was a political economy that also tipped toward art, a political economy already modified by its engagement with *la question sociale* and its creation of *économie sociale*, that received institutional space and status in French law faculties after 1877. It was a more dubious political economy that emerged victorious after 1877.

While the invention of *économie sociale* as a place to confine *la question sociale* had profound effects on the discipline of political economy itself, it also had far-reaching and profound effects upon French society in general. And in fact, by the end of the nineteenth century, *économie sociale* seems to have taken on a life of its own, with boundaries that political economists could no longer police, with definitions and implications that economists could no longer regulate, and with practitioners who economists no longer recognized as economists. Having escaped political economy's efforts to keep it close and thus useful, the discourse that was social economy began to thrive and to proliferate, with productive, creative, and dynamic consequences.

This explosion of *économie sociale* contrasted quite notably, however, with the declining interest shown to social economy by the most familiar organizations of French political economy. The *Journal des économistes* and the *Annales de la Société d'économie politique*, for instance, only rarely featured discussions of *la question sociale* by the first decade of the twentieth century. The factory towns, housing projects, and working-class conditions that added vital topics of discussion–not to mention color–to these economic journals seem to have become of less interest or concern to economists by the end of the century. One of the last real descriptions of a paternalist factory town appeared in the *Journal des économistes* in 1882, and the paternalist projects displayed at the 1889 and 1900 World's Fair as a panacea for *la question sociale* only temporarily reinvigorated economists' discussions of labor management.[26] Similarly, discussions of *économie sociale* disappeared from the *Journal* almost altogether. Other than references to social economy in the context of the World's Fairs exhibits, one of the last explicit discussions in the *Journal* of the relationship between political and social economy was in 1887.[27] Admittedly, the relationship between *économie politique* and *économie sociale*, or between the science and art of political economy, did remain an object of concern in the 1891 *Nouveau dictionnaire d'économie politique*, but it is clear that these discussions occurred without the intensity, frequency, and originality of the mid-century debates, and no longer within the heart of French political economy.

And yet by the end of the nineteenth century, everywhere but among the traditional zones of *économie politique*, there was an explosion of people, journals, academic posts, and institutions, all either employing the term *économie sociale*, or investigating topics and questions that could be deemed "social economic" in nature. In French universities, in particular, social economy appears to have multiplied. In 1898, the *Faculté de droit de Paris* created a course in *économie sociale* granted to Charles Gide; several years later the course was transformed into a chair.[28] In 1893, at the *Conservatoire des arts et métiers*, a course in commercial law was turned into a chair of *droit commercial et économie sociale* [commercial law and social economy], and the chair conferred upon Paul Beauregard, who himself would go on to replace Paul Cauwès at the *Faculté de droit de Paris* as professor of *économie politique*. The chair of *droit commercial et économie sociale* was, in 1894, split in two, creating separate courses in commercial law and social economy.[29] Social economic concerns would continue to flourish at the *Conservatoire*: in the years after 1900, the school created a chair in *assurance et prévoyance sociale* [insurance and social providence], a chair in the history of labor, and finally, a chair in the *histoire des associations ouvrières* [history of working-class associations].[30] In 1893 at the *École libre des sciences politiques*, or *Sciences-Po*, Émile Cheysson, who had taught a course in *économie politique* since 1883, began teaching a course on *questions ouvrières en France et à l'étranger* [working-class issues in France and abroad].[31] In 1900, that course was renamed *économie sociale*, with Cheysson continuing to teach it.[32]

Most significant, perhaps, of the eruptions of social economy in academia was the creation in 1893 of a chair in the *histoire d'économie sociale* [history of social economy] at the *Faculté de Lettres de Paris*, a chair that is widely claimed by historians of sociology to be the first explicitly sociological course at the Sorbonne.[33] There is no better evidence of social economy's status *not* as a discipline, but as a "sensibility,"[34] something that could inform or rub off on other disciplines, other discourses, or other institutions. It hardly matters whether sociologists meant the same thing by *économie sociale* as economists, or whether a course in *économie sociale* taught at the Sorbonne looked exactly the same as a course in *économie sociale* taught at the *École des Mines* or the *Conservatoire des arts et métiers*. What matters instead is the proliferation of *économie sociale* by the end of the century, the overlap between *économie sociale* and a variety of other disciplines (such as law, sociology, criminology, social work), the infusion of *économie sociale* into disciplines that were *not*, in fact, labeled "social economy." The significance of these new chairs and courses devoted to *économie sociale* in French academia lies in what they reveal about the metamorphic power of the discourse of social economy. By the end of the century, no one controlled the discourse; no one controlled or even patrolled its boundaries; no single discipline, and no single profession, could claim it as theirs and theirs alone.

Économie sociale flourished outside academia as well, particularly in a "parapolitical sphere" which historian Janet Horne has defined as existing "in the interstices of government, philanthropy, and industry, midway between the public interests of the state and the private interests of individuals."[35] A quick parade of the institutions, professional groups, and periodicals that employed the term *économie sociale*, took up the discourse, or tackled some of the problems and solutions so often collected under the rubric of *économie sociale*, suggests the incredible propagation of the discourse. Engineer and sociologist Frédéric Le Play founded the *Société d'économie sociale* in 1856, and launched the journal *La Réforme sociale* in 1881.[36] The discourse of social economy was also on display at the Universal Exhibition in Paris in 1867 where a new exhibit was organized, the focus of which was not things, but rather people and their happiness.[37] Labeled the Tenth Group, the exhibit displayed paternalist projects, whose ultimate goals were the creation of a moral industrial society, harmony between employers and employees, and public peace and social order.[38] The identification of *la question sociale* as *the* social problem *par excellence*, and the display of the heretofore most popular solution to *la question sociale*, marked the 1867 Exhibition as a concrete site of the proliferation of *économie sociale*. Social economy continued to thrive at the World Exhibitions, with social economy sections at both the 1889 and the

1900 Exhibitions. The 1889 Exhibition was also notable as a precursor to the *Musée Social*, founded in 1894 as an institution dedicated to the non-socialist, non-revolutionary solution of *la question sociale*.

Frédéric Le Play; *La Réforme Sociale*; the 1867, 1889, and 1900 Universal Exhibitions; the *Musée Social*: all have significant histories of their own that have been told with great skill. But what matters here, quite simply, is the manner in which the parapolitical sphere, parallel to the academic sphere, experienced an extraordinary explosion of the discourse of *économie sociale* within an incredible variety of institutions, social organizations, periodicals, extra-governmental bodies, and think-tanks, all employing the term, the vocabulary, the themes, the concerns—in short, the discourse—of *économie sociale*. And again, as in academia, there was no single entity—no single organization, no single institution, no single individual, no single discipline—that controlled the parameters of that discourse.

Recently, sociologist Christian Topalov has referred to a *fin-de-siècle* "reformist nebula," frequented by a variety of individuals, from a variety of social backgrounds, political affiliations, and social concerns, all connected by a common-sense belief in the need for reform and a skepticism toward governmental non-involvement:

> The metaphor of the 'nebula' suggests the task to be accomplished: to explore a finite universe, but one with undefined contours, an intermittent subject composed of dense nuclei and relatively empty zones, of bodies in the process of formation or disintegration, an ensemble of objects organized into partial systems but carried along in a movement of the whole.[39]

Topalov notes that the flexibility of his definition mirrors the flexibility of the nebula itself, thus making it possible to talk about the *fin-de-siècle* impulse toward reform without getting distracted by the individual peculiarities of particular reformers, reforming institutions, or reforming stimuli. The *nébuleuse réformatrice* was a field of engagement, onto and through which a variety of individuals and groups moved in an unrehearsed and uncoordinated plan of action. Topalov is making, in other words, an argument about the *nébuleuse réformatrice* quite similar to the argument that I have made about *économie sociale*.

For Topalov, however, social economy was a *science*, "a science of social progress" and thus a participant in and contributor to the reforming nebula, but a science that ultimately failed in its efforts at institutionalization.[40] He is the latest, then, in a long line of scholars examining *économie sociale* who have tried to give it real and defined contours, a concrete identity, and real disciplinary status. But what happens instead if we take Topalov's definition of *la nébuleuse réformatrice*, with its flexible borders, its intermittence, its dynamism, and apply it to social economy? What if we argue that *économie sociale*, far from being a discipline that functioned as part of a reforming nebula, *was* the reforming nebula? That *économie sociale was* the flexible, intermittent, dynamic, endlessly shifting field of engagement that contained all those efforts to engage with *la question sociale*? The historical significance of *économie sociale*, then, lies in the fact that it did *not* become a distinct discipline; that it did not gain institutional status; that despite the failed efforts to permanently institutionalize it, the discourse of *économie sociale* nonetheless thrived, having proven itself essential. The central irony within the history of nineteenth-century French political economy was that it was political economy's *detritus*—rather than political economy itself—that has been most successful, that has flourished, that has proven both socially indispensable and historically enduring.

Governmentality, *la question sociale*, and *économie sociale*

As the umbrella category that held all discussions of *la question sociale*, social economy could only have proliferated, infused other disciplines, captured new supporters, and motivated new policies—in short, taken on a life of its own—if *la question sociale* were still a problem of momentous social import requiring proper solution. Social economy's flourishing suggested that *la question sociale* was no closer to successful resolution by the end of the century than at the beginning. Why had *la question sociale* not been solved despite the many efforts since the 1830s to find a solution? Why was *économie sociale* thriving? And what were the consequences of *not* having solved the social question? All these questions point in the direction of governmentality, that neologism coined by Michel Foucault to refer to a new way of thinking about power, about the techniques or practices of power, and about the aims of governmental practice.

To understand what Foucault and others have meant by "governmentality" first requires exploring what they have meant by "government."[41] In witty but typically ambiguous fashion, Foucault referred to government as the "conduct of conduct." Clarifying Foucault's quip, sociologist Mitchell Dean defines government as "any more or less calculated means of the direction of how we behave and act,"[42] and notes that government is an inherently plural activity, with multiple agents, multiple aims, and multiple means; it is an activity that is not confined to agents or agencies of the state proper.[43] Government tends to work through what Dean refers to as "practices of the self." In other words, the "conduct of conduct" tends to shape human behavior by relying upon individuals, and their "choices, desires, aspirations, needs, wants and lifestyles,"[44] as the primary agents of government.

If government refers to a set of practices designed to shape human conduct, governmentality refers both to the particular way a society *thinks* about government (that is, thinks about the shaping of human conduct), and an historically specific form of that thinking about government. If government entails practice or art, governmentality entails practice/art conjoined with thought. And the type of governmentality by which Foucault and others have been most intrigued is a particular form of thinking about and exercising power that emerged over the course of the seventeenth and eighteenth centuries alongside the realization that the population represented a natural resource that the state could not ignore and needed to cultivate. Governmentality, then, was the particular thinking about the "conduct of conduct" that treated the population—and more specifically, the health, welfare, and productivity of the population—as something that required management. That particular form of governmentality, and its particular objectives, gave rise to specific techniques for shaping the conduct of the population according to the basic requirement of a healthy and productive population. Those techniques themselves comprise what Mitchell Dean refers to as "apparatuses of security," which include:

> the use of standing armies, police forces, diplomatic corps, intelligence services and spies. It also includes health, education and social welfare systems and the mechanisms of the management of the national economy. It thus encompasses those institutions and practices concerned to defend, maintain and secure a national population and those that secure the economic, demographic and social processes that are found to exist within that population....Rather than replacing discipline or sovereignty, the modern art of government recasts them within this concern for the population and its optimization (in terms of wealth, health, happiness, prosperity, efficiency), and the forms of knowledge and technical means appropriate to it.[45]

Bio-power—another Foucauldian neologism often used as a synonym for governmentality—is the power of life, the power to keep life, the power to preserve and cultivate life. But to cultivate the life of the population—to keep the population healthy, productive, safe, long-lived—requires information about that population: about the specific problems suffered by that population; about the effects of those particular problems; about the best ways to solve those problems and alleviate that suffering depending upon the specific populations in question; about the variable success rates of particular solutions; and about the relative success of the administering agents of those solutions. And it is in the collection of information that the human sciences cooperate. If governmentality entails the combination of practice with thought, the human sciences offer some of the forms of knowledge that come to be employed in the art of government.[46] As the human sciences—psychology, social work, criminology, sociology, and political economy, to name just a few—collect more information about their subjects in order to know more about them and thus keep them (or make them) healthy and productive, this knowledge makes possible greater regulation of those subjects, whether in the form of explicit rules, laws, or policies, or in the form of equally regulatory tactics of normalization.

Governmentality represents, then, a new way of thinking about power unlike traditional ways, in which questions about power are questions about its legitimacy or illegitimacy. Traditional ways of thinking about power assume that power is visible, and that individuals who are ruled are capable of clearly seeing and understanding the operations of power, and thus determining for themselves whether they have consented to legitimate power or not. Governmentality, in contrast, represents a type of power that is *not* immediately visible, and that is not consented to. It is a type of power that is neither exclusively held nor exercised by the state, and that usually operates outside the arena of the state, below the level of laws, rights, and judicial protection for those rights. It lacks the traditional "look" of power, which operates visibly from the top down, as a negative presence that prevents or represses. Instead, governmentality is a type of power that studies, reveals, collects, and produces. It is a type of power that weaves throughout society, operating so effectively because its agents do not appear to be agents of power and because its subjects are not necessarily aware of its operations. The net result of governmentality, of the spread of this modern form of power, is that while most of us may feel as if we enjoy more rights, more protection, and more liberty, we are simultaneously better known, better regulated, and more subject to tactics of normalization than populations at any other moment in history.

One of the corollaries of this book's genealogy of the dubious science of political economy is the exposure of that particular human science's unintentional and fitful cooperation with this new art of government whose central aim was the management of the welfare of the population. The history of French political economy, and in particular its awkward relationship with *la question sociale* and social economy, exposes something about the historical shift toward a particular type of power and a particular art of government. The rest of this chapter, then, will explore a series of questions, the answers to which reveal political and social economy's entanglement with this peculiarly modern way of thinking about the conduct of conduct.[47] First, if social economy was a form of knowledge pulled into and informing government, who was the entity to be governed using that form of knowledge? Second, how did political and social economy make possible a particular way of thinking, which consequently informed particular practices operating on workers, industrialists, and the economy? Third, what was *wanted*, what was *desired*, from those who came to be governed by the agents and agencies employing political and social economy as particular forms of knowledge? And finally, who or what was granted authority by the collection, analysis and use of information that constituted "the doing of social economy"?

Through the lens of governmentality, *économie sociale* can be understood as a form of knowledge that informed and infused the techniques used, and the purposes sought, by both state and extra-state authorities and agencies engaged in the shaping of the conduct of those engaged in labor, whether workers *or* employers. During the nineteenth century, *la question sociale* gave rise to an interconnected regime of practices and a network of forms of knowledge all engaged in the relief of poverty and social misery. The regime of practices linked a variety of institutions and techniques: factories and paternalism; government agencies and welfare provisions; universities, their academic posts, and the knowledge they collected, produced, and disseminated; state-funded think-tanks like the *Académie des sciences morales et politiques*, and extra-state (or para-political) ones like the *Musée social*. This regime of practices informed, was reshaped by, and gave rise to, various forms of knowledge. Political economy and social economy were two of those forms of knowledge.

Political economy, in the early nineteenth century, had proposed particular strategies for government, all of which could be collected into the phrase *laissez-faire*. For early nineteenth-century economists, government was something that ought to be left to individuals themselves. *Laissez-faire* meant not simply staying out of the economy, but out of the individual choices, decisions, and responsibilities which fed the workings of the economy. The empirical knowledge thrown up by *la question sociale*, however, transformed what political economy could say about government. Political economists' understanding of the population as a natural resource bound up with the wealth of nations dovetailed with governmentality, that is, with the notion that the health and welfare of the population were an appropriate aim of state and focus of government practices. But economists' competing goals, in particular the immediate desire to protect their supposedly natural, universal science and its pretensions to truth, and thus their professional ambitions, clashed with the imperatives of governmentality. Their invention of *économie sociale*, then, was designed as a place to hide, to sequester *la question sociale* and what it implied about the need for the government of the population, and the management, regulation, and government of the system of industrial capitalism and the economy itself. Social economy became a protected space to ponder *la question sociale* and what it suggested about populations, individuals, discipline, management, regulation, and assistance; to ponder, in short, what *la question sociale* suggested about government. Once political economists lost control of *économie sociale*, it was launched independently, without its creators and overseers, into the network of practices and knowledge enveloping the study and relief of poverty and social misery.

Social economy was a form of knowledge that offered information, posed questions, and proffered answers that highlighted the misery, rather than the health, of the population. It was a form of knowledge that proposed solutions for how to improve the welfare and optimize the prosperity and efficiency of the working-class population: paternalism, government regulation, self-discipline, education, religion, to name just a few. It offered information at odds with political economists' traditional depiction of the economy as self-regulating and harmonious, and of industrial capitalism as offering an equal opportunity for social mobility and economic advancement for anyone who seized it. Social economy was a form of knowledge that undermined conventional understandings of how the economy worked; how it behaved; how, when, and with what effects it responded either to adjustments or upheavals. Social economy suggested simultaneously that misery was not irrefutable proof of immorality—that even the most moral of workers might still feel misery—and that the industrial capitalist economy could *not* be predicted, whether by economists or, more importantly, by the workers who were supposed to be prepared for its vicissitudes. If the economy was not predictable; if it was not self-regulating; if it was not harmonious, then the misery of French workers could not be attributed to immoral and foolish behavior, could not be alleviated through the experience of misery itself, and could not be dismissed as a temporary dilemma.

Social economy made particular issues and problems governable that political economy could not. If *laissez-faire* was inherently at odds with much of what constituted the modern art of government, social economy opened up the possibility of that art in an arena once closed to it. Social economy made it possible, even necessary, to think of workers as people who required government, who were incapable of self-government without prior assistance or training. More importantly, *économie sociale* made it possible, even necessary, to consider self-government as impossible to accomplish within the context of a global industrial capitalist economy, in which global events could have profound effects that no one could plan for, no matter how prepared, prudent, and moral.

If *économie sociale* made it possible to think of Labor, of French workers, as necessarily subject to government, it also make it possible to think of industrialists, those people most directly "governing" Labor, as equally in need of government. As early as the 1830s, political economists had expressed a cautious dismay at the fine line between the rights of private enterprise and outright greed and callousness among industrialists. If certain industrialists, such as those of the Industrial Society of Mulhouse, had voluntarily assumed the burden of alleviating the worst excesses of workers' misery, there were others who had adopted behavior toward their workers that was at best indifferent and imprudent, and at worst, downright immoral. Social economy thus made it possible to imagine that something, or someone, might need to step in and artificially level the playing field between workers and industrialists, constraining what free enterprise entailed. Social economy, in fact, created the space to recognize what Adam Smith had once argued in *The Wealth of Nations*, that the interests of workers and employers, as well as their respective bargaining positions, were seldom identical, and that employers usually operated from positions of greater strength, advantage, and authority than workers.[48]

But to govern workers and industrialists, to assist the former and constrain the latter, was by definition to govern the industrial capitalist economy. At its core, *économie sociale* was a critique of the assumptions that the economy was balanced and harmonious; that its laws were, in fact, laws; that its effects were indiscriminately beneficial; and that as participants in the economy, individuals *were* individuals, rather than industrialists who owned the means of production, exercised the right to vote, and enjoyed large reserves of capital, or workers with nothing but their labor power, living from paycheck to paycheck, without the right to vote, to organize, to meet in assembly, or to strike. Social economy was a form of knowledge that envisioned the economy, not simply as something that *could* be governed by human intervention, but something that *ought* to be governed. The dangerous nature of this critique explains why political economists had to keep it away from their science, sequester it, monitor its boundaries, and keep it from contaminating and corroding their own form of knowledge.

It was through the lens and the discourse of social economy that it was possible to imagine, propose, and implement laws protecting women's and children's labor: the number of hours these workers could work, the type of labor they could do, the industries in which they could or could not work, the type of supervision under which they could work. It was through the lens of social economy—according to which workers and industrialists did not share the same interests—that it was possible to envision factory inspectors, whose job it was to assure that the laws protecting and regulating the welfare of workers were being respected by industrialists. It was through the lens of social economy that it was possible to consider accidents as an inherent risk of industrial production rather than the results of personal failing, and thus their solution to be a collective social task, rather than an individual one. Social economy made it possible to imagine practices like paternalism, and to extend that vision to the proposal of state-sponsored welfare programs. In other words, if industrialists could mitigate the unpredictability of the economy by helping workers through moments of misery, then perhaps the state could mitigate that unpredictability more consistently and more effectively. Social economy made it possible to imagine that if workers required *government*, that government could be more effective through practices that felt less like discipline and more like pleasurable persuasion: education, free-time, professional training, leisure activities, leisure spaces.

As part of the matrix of governmentality, social economy pointed at possible strategies for assuring the health and welfare of people defined as workers. The practices of government to which social economy offered validation were practices designed to create docile, mute, productive, stable, and moral bodies out of supposedly disobedient, unproductive, and immoral ones. The desired attributes of French workers were thus the same attributes that industrialists had sought to achieve with early nineteenth-century paternalism. Social economy provided not simply a means for imagining, and thus validating, industrial paternalism in the mid-nineteenth century, but for the co-opting of these paternalist practices by the state by the end of the nineteenth century. And thus, we are back at the idea of paternalism—which is, quite simply, a regime of governmental practices—as a productive system of power, productive of particular types of potentialities, capabilities, and capacities, and of workers who were resources rather than menaces. Social economy gave license to, and provided evidence of, the successful functioning of governmental practices—whether implemented by industrialists or by agents of the state—that relied upon "practices of the self," practices that attempted to shape workers into self-disciplining, self-governing subjects.[49] The provision of education, job training, clean and comfortable housing, gardens: these were practices designed not simply with the short-term strategy of alleviating immediate misery, but with the long-term strategy of encouraging workers to think of themselves as people who *could* live like this; of encouraging workers to see and understand the benefits of behaving and thus living this way; and of encouraging workers to communicate this way of thinking, behaving, and living to the next generation.

Finally, as a form of knowledge that encompassed *la question sociale*, social economy initially confirmed political economists—those men doing social economy—as experts in Labor. Social economy was a space for political economists to proffer a different type of information about workers, different than the information they could proffer as economists committed to their universal science. Social economy allowed economists to claim privileged knowledge of workers, and of how the mechanisms of the economy affected the daily lives of workers. But of course the expertise that social economy confirmed upon economists was a double-edged sword. Social economy confirmed economists as analysts of the mechanisms of the economy and of the social consequences of the economy, but challenged the basic foundations of the way they understood the mechanisms of the economy.

And as social economy escaped the control of political economists, and as the discourse proliferated and was used in ways unintended by economists, it also validated the work of experts who were not economists: social workers, analysts of family dynamics; criminologists, specialists in criminal behavior and in the social circumstances that contributed to crime; sociologists, authorities in the analysis of social structures and social organization; public hygienists, experts in public health and the control of disease. These experts were given license to observe, to collect data, to inspect, and to propose. In short, they were given license to make visible particular individuals, their problems, and the lived consequences of those problems, all under the rubric of that endlessly changing category of *économie sociale*, and all under the impulse of solving *la question sociale*.

One of the more interesting contributions to the European historical literature in the last few decades has been the work on the almost obsessive nineteenth-century preoccupation with sex, sexual problems, and sexual "abnormalities" which would seem to contradict the usual depiction of Victorian Europe as sexually repressed.[50] Historians have argued that something called "sexuality" was actually the *effect* of the constant investigations into people's sexual practices, of the constant incitements to self-discipline vis-à-vis sex, and of the constant incitements to discussion about individual and collective sexual practice. Just as it was an effect of power, however, sexuality was also an *instrument* of power. It was a site of the subtle spreading of regulatory strategies and disciplinary techniques, of the collection of information about populations, and of the formation of academic disciplines interested in the health of populations and individuals.

La question sociale can be understood in the same way: as a grand, overarching, poorly-defined, poorly-delimited but easily-identified, catchily-named problem that enabled the collection of information and the spread of disciplinary techniques; that aided in the creation and protection of academic disciplines that purported to study this problem; and that focused contemporaries' attention on certain people and certain issues, and diverted their attention from others. If there was during the nineteenth century an extraordinary explosion of discourse about sex, there was also an explosion of discourse about *la question sociale*, an explosion that often occurred under the rubric of *économie sociale*. As I have already argued, this explosion of discourse about *la question sociale* opened the opportunity for the collection of information about French workers, their living conditions, their private behaviors, their motivations (or lack thereof), and their failings. The explosion of discourse about *la question sociale* offered to older academic disciplines (law, psychiatry, psychology, medicine) the possibility of new jurisdictional claims, and lent credibility to a variety of newer disciplines (social work, public hygiene, criminology, sociology).

But just as particularly worrisome sexual problems proved unsolvable, so did *la question sociale* appear unresolved by 1900 despite almost a century of investigation, discussion, and attempted solution. Industrialists, economists, social observers, social scientists and politicians discussing *la question sociale* late in the nineteenth century seemed no more confident that the problem was waning, or that proper solutions had been devised, than industrialists, economists, social observers, and politicians fifty years earlier. While there is no doubt that many French industrialists, politicians, socialists, economists, reformers, and philanthropists desperately wanted to solve *la question sociale*—or have it solved for them—if only because their own interests required its solution, it is nonetheless significant that *not* solving it presented as many opportunities, particularly for the operations of power, as actually solving it.

The failure of the effort to solve *la question sociale*, and thus the continued relevance and proliferation of social economy as the discourse and space that professed to study it, opened up opportunities that contributed to the spread of extra-governmental power and regulation—to the spread, in other words, of governmentality—into French society. The failure of efforts to solve *la question sociale* afforded continuous justification for discussion of the working-class "problem," and for the interventionist, regulatory, and normalizing policies of the industrial class, the Church, social organizations, the human sciences, as well as the state. Failure allowed the French state to demand that yet *more* information be collected about the working class; it allowed new disciplines like psychiatry, social work, and criminology new justifications for the continued observation, study, measurement, analysis, and expert appraisal of the French working class; it allowed for yet more debate over *économie sociale*, and yet more opportunities for its proliferation. Failure to solve *la question sociale* sanctioned yet more regulation of the workplace, of workers' housing, of industrial practices; it allowed for yet more discussion of what could be considered "normal" (working conditions, living conditions, family life, political involvement, etc.) and what could be considered "abnormal" (working conditions, living conditions, family life, political involvement, etc.). Failure to solve *la question sociale* authorized the spread of yet more disciplinary practices (implemented by industrialists, by the State, by reform agencies, by local authorities), and incited yet more self-discipline among workers, more self-help, more moderation of their choices, aspirations, and desires. The net result of these efforts to solve *la question sociale*, of their presumed failure, and hence, of the yet more impassioned demands to work even harder to solve the problem, was that the French working class was more regulated in 1900 than it had been in 1830, was better known, more thoroughly investigated by social scientists, and more thoroughly "understood" by public opinion. The gaze that efforts to solve *la question sociale* had directed toward workers—a gaze in which political economists were complicit—had rendered French workers more visible than they had ever been. The longer efforts to solve *la question sociale* remained apparent failures, the further the discourse of *économie sociale* spread, and the more visible French workers became. And thus the consequence of the failure to solve *la question sociale* was an unparalleled expansion and diffusion of regulatory power under the guise of help and knowledge.

The argument I have made in this chapter is quasi-causal, but eminently non-subjective. Of all the human sciences developing during the nineteenth century which informed the care, management, and health of both individuals and populations, of all the human sciences participating in a web of welfare and regulation, political economy was the *least* likely to intentionally and unproblematically collaborate with interventionist, regulatory, and normalizing practices. As practitioners of a discipline older than sociology, social work, or criminology, political economists were less willing for much longer to admit its "social" status, modeling their discipline as they did on the physical sciences. The history of French political economy during the nineteenth century is the history of political economists trying to hold off the participation of their discipline in the "conduct of conduct." That economists failed; and yet that their failure was *productive*; that they unleashed a discourse that was swept up in the matrix of governmentality and that contributed to particular ways of thinking about the regulation and management of workers, industrialists, even the economy itself, was unintentional, unexpected, and unwanted.

But as this book has explored, the history of French political economy during the nineteenth century is also the history of economists' efforts to *prove*—to the French state, to institutions of higher education, and to public opinion—that theirs was a *useful* science, that economists provided socially-useful knowledge, that their science had practical, daily, lived consequences for all members of society. Ironically, though, in historical hindsight it has been the *detritus* of political economy, the material political economy sloughed off in order to continue to promote its claims to be a science of broad, social significance, that has truly mattered, that has produced real effects for real human beings. The discipline of economics in France may well have secured a place within the walls of academia, but perhaps—as the proponents of Post-Autistic Economics would agree—at the cost of their claims to provide socially-useful knowledge of broad social consequence. The most socially-useful knowledge that political economy provided came *not* from the heart of the economic discipline, but from all those social questions that political economy had tried to corral in its pursuit of professional status and legitimacy. Over the nineteenth century, the utility of political economy—claimed by economists for their discipline itself—shifted to that area *outside* the discipline, to its residual, to all those things left over and outside the parameters of political economy in its search for "scientific" status. The history of nineteenth-century French political economy is a perfect example, then, of Foucault's warning, quoted once before, that "people know what they do; they frequently know why they do what they do; but what they don't know is what what they do does."[51]

Conclusion

As an epitaph for nineteenth-century French political economy, Louis Reybaud's 1841 statement would serve well: "Like all human knowledge, political economy has its doubts, its miscalculations, its chasms."[1] In these pages I have narrated a particular moment in the history of French political economy, a moment of profound doubt, and a particularly hazardous obstacle in political economy's path toward certainty: the obstacle represented by *la question sociale.* If we continue to take seriously some of the themes that this book has treated—the appearance of *la question sociale* as a disciplinary dilemma faced by French political economy; the invention and utility of *économie sociale* by and for political economy; the escape and proliferation of social economy outside the auspices of political economy; the productive failure of *la question sociale*—what work still needs to be done to trace these themes to the present? I hope that in this conclusion I can convince others to pursue these questions, to pursue the history of the dubious science of political economy, as well as the implications of that history, into the present.

This book has explored the nineteenth-century history of the "dubious" science of political economy, a label that, as should now be clear, economists themselves would have rejected, and from which they tried to protect themselves throughout the nineteenth century through a complex array of discursive and institutional practices. The nineteenth-century history of French political economy was a history of unwelcome and unanticipated movement away from the supposedly heroic scientific qualities of the early nineteenth-century discipline[2]; away from certainty; away from the supposedly revolutionary potential of political economy to uncover economic mechanisms that stemmed from Nature; away from a belief in the unfailingly fair, balanced, and self-regulating laws of the economy, laws that mimicked those of planetary motion in their universality and lack of ambiguity. Much to their dismay, nineteenth-century political economists were forced to acknowledge that economic "laws" were profoundly different than those of the hard sciences; that abstraction in physics looked different in economics, in which the category of Labor served to conveniently mask what were, in fact, real human beings; that experimentation in economics could only be speculation rather than pure calculation, and necessarily relied upon knowledge of a past that was contingent rather than inescapable; that there was no social consensus about allowing economic "laws" to unfold to their logical end without social intervention or social assistance; and that the human element in political economy was inescapable and usually unpredictable. For French political economists, *la question sociale* was not only the problem of what to do with people left unmoored by economic developments, or of how to best manage the unanticipated crises brought about by rapid industrialization, or of how to remedy the problems of unemployment, ill health, insufficient wages, and class conflict. *La question sociale* was also a theoretical dilemma for political economists: for the presumably certain nature of their own science; for the way they had understood themselves as scientists; and for the social role that they had understood themselves as necessarily playing in, and the contributions they were making to, French society. *La question sociale* was the social problem that forced economists to face the fact that their "science" was far more dubious than they wanted to admit.

Despite French economists' best efforts to keep *la question sociale* under wraps (so to speak) by quarantining it within the invented category of *économie sociale*, thus protecting the basic scientific qualities and tenets of their discipline and allowing it to achieve institutional success within French law schools, *la question sociale* and *économie sociale* ultimately escaped their control. Economists may have kept the social question out of economics proper, but they could not keep it out of public discourse more generally. By the early twentieth century, the discipline of French political economy had theoretically rejected *la question sociale* but had been unable to keep itself free of the influence of social economy, the category economists had invented to house *la question sociale* and all its implications. In fact, as *la question sociale* and *économie sociale* permeated public discourse, few social sciences remained untouched. The gap between political economy's efforts to be a "hard" science, and what economists increasingly understood, or admitted, their science to be—a social science, a human science, a dubious science—was evidenced by the company that political economy kept by the end of the century. While early nineteenth-century political economists aspired to the fellowship of chemists, mathematicians, and physicists, later in the century they were keeping company with a host of other social scientists all engaging with *la question sociale*: psychologists, psychiatrists, criminologists, sociologists, urban planners, public hygienists, medical scientists, and lawyers.

By 1900, then, French political economy had recognized its own dubiousness. Pursuing the history of French political economy into the twentieth century, however, historian Lucette Le Van-Lemesle has narrated another moment, beginning in the 1930s and lasting until the 1950s, in which French economics, under attack for having lost its scientific rigor, attempted a new effort at "self-scientificization." With the Great Depression of the 1930s, French economics came under particular attack from students and professors at the *École polytechnique*, for whom the training provided to students of economics at the *facultés de droit* lacked a sufficient foundation in mathematics and statistics, understood to be exact sciences and thus crucial elements in the achievement of disciplinary precision and exactness.[3] The history of twentieth-century political economy, then, would appear to be a history of both rupture and continuation. On the one hand, rupture with nineteenth-century political economy's recognition—however uncomfortable and unwanted—that its subject was as much the human beings who lived within the orbit of supposedly natural universal economic laws as it was the mechanism of those laws themselves. But on the other hand, continuation as well: with the problem of how to squeeze social questions out of the discipline of political economy; of how to eradicate the dubious scientificity of the discipline and affiliate with the hard and exact sciences; and of how to make cast-iron laws, statistics, and mathematical models the appropriate subject of economic attention, rather than the ambiguity and imprecision—the messiness—of lived economic experience.

For the second time I quote political economist Théodore Fix, writing in an 1845 article in the *Journal des économistes*:

> Without a doubt, political economy, considered in the most restrained and strict sense of the word, is nothing but the science of the production of wealth....But when the practical consequences and results of its [formulas and laws] are examined, one encounters man facing you, man with his needs, tendencies and passions. Thus, political economy is no longer this simple science that unfolds in an inflexible manner in a series of axioms and propositions. It finds itself grappling with the most diverse interests, with social necessities, with morality, with politics, even with the difference of conditions and intelligence, and finally with institutions, practices and traditions.[4]

Here Fix set forth the challenge that French political economy faced in the nineteenth century, and the challenge that by the mid-twentieth century, French economists tried, yet again, to counter with a call to abstraction and to numbers, and with an emphasis upon the scientificity and neutrality of the economic discipline. This book has demonstrated, however, that the nineteenth-century process of grappling with "man with his needs, tendencies and passions" was far from straightforward. Twentieth-century French political economy faced—and continues, into the twenty-first century, to face—similar problems. The contemporary challenge to the "autism" of the abstract mathematical and statistical economics taught in France (as elsewhere), bears out this claim.

Whether or not, however, this boundary between the discipline of economics and social issues—what in the nineteenth century was given the broad label of *la question sociale*—has been breached, and whatever the degree of that breach at any given time (that is, how much of the social question gets let back in, or manages to squeeze back in), that boundary—between things economic and things social, between the study of the supposed laws of the economy and actual social events and effects, between mathematical economic models and real economic actors—has historically been *definitional to the discipline*. That boundary has been, and still is, crucial to the way that economics has understood itself, and to the way that economics has fought on its own behalf professionally and institutionally. The Post-Autistics Economics movement is presently challenging that boundary, and those fighting to protect economics from this challenge are massing precisely on that same boundary: between that which is economic (and thus predictable, measurable, amoral, natural, universal and unregulated) and that which is social (and thus unpredictable, unmeasurable, historical, and governed). It is not the answer to the question "is economics an exact science or a dubious one?" that is most significant, but rather the question itself, and the manner in which, at least in France, that question has historically followed the discipline and its practitioners, and has constrained its professional efforts and its claims to legitimacy.

To put it another way, if the answer to the question "is economics an exact or dubious science?" *is* significant, it is significant for the type of answer given to the question at different historical moments. If the boundary between the economic and the social—and the processes of establishing that boundary, protecting it, questioning it, moving it, challenging it—has been historically definitional to the discipline of political economy in France, that boundary has shifted historically. And yet, it is usually *not* a feature of the histories that disciplines tell about themselves to illuminate those boundary shifts, to reveal former uncertainties, to uncover changing opinions, or to point out might-have-beens. Hence, the utility of this genealogical investigation, which has uncovered a very different history of French political economy during the nineteenth century than the comfortable one of slow-and-steady linear development toward a hard, exact science. And thus the relevance of asking whether contemporary discussions of economics in Europe have uncovered the similarity between the current critiques of economics and nineteenth-century critiques of the same aspirations to disciplinary scientificity, precision, and exactness at the expense of "man with his needs, tendencies and passions." If the answer is no, why not? What has happened to those nineteenth-century struggles with *la question sociale* in the history that French economists tell about themselves and their discipline? Have those struggles been (conveniently) forgotten (or repressed? or disqualified? or excluded?)? Why, and how? To what effect, and to whose benefit? The genealogical technique of uncovering "subjugated knowledges," used here on the nineteenth-century history of French political economy, thus bears repeating on its more recent histories.

If the story of nineteenth-century political economy and its engagement with *la question sociale* has offered some insight into the way academic disciplines construct, re-construct, and forget their pasts, identify and re-identify disciplinary goals, and engage with institutional structures and power hierarchies in order to achieve status, this story also has implications for historians' study of the broad subject of governmentality. The boundary between the economic and the social, and the historical struggle either to breach or defend that boundary, connects political economy to a history of thinking about human populations as resources of the state, as human capital whose health and welfare are instrumental to the health and welfare of the state itself. That boundary between the economic and the social, between political economy and *la question sociale* was, and still is, the foundation for governmentality. If the cultivation of human resources is central to the new forms of power which Michel Foucault labeled governmentality, the history of French political economy, even as the discipline was defending its claim to be an exact, methodical, inflexible, and mathematical science, is a history of engagement–in the sense of becoming entangled–with governmentality. Far from isolating itself from the practices of government, the discipline of political economy relied, and continues to rely, upon the network of state and extra-state agencies not only for its data and statistical evidence, but for a public arena in which the discipline can take a stand on significant issues, recommend policy, and claim legitimacy, status, and power.

One of the most significant implications of Foucault's work on governmentality is the implicit warning against the claim that there can be a *real* social science, that is, a social science that does not intersect with modern forms of power, that has actually been able to separate itself from political concerns and practices, that can study human populations with the same type of detachment used by mathematicians solving a proof. *Can* the social sciences ever free themselves from discipline, normalization, confession, and examination? Foucault would have argued no. But the history of French political economy is the history of precisely that struggle, of that negotiation between economists' claim and desire to be practitioners of an exact science in the mold of mathematics, chemistry and physics, and their recognition of the human, lived, real implications of their presumably scientific study. Early nineteenth-century French political economists claimed to be exact scientists, only to be faced, by mid-century, with *la question sociale* and everything that particular challenge represented for their "science." If contemporary neo-classical economists, with their attachment to mathematics, have again attempted—through yet another appeal to "science"—to separate themselves from political concerns and practices, has that attempt worked? Has twenty-first century economic social "science" freed itself from discipline, normalization, confession, and examination? Has it achieved something that nineteenth-century economics could not? The historical significance of the challenge on behalf of lived economic situations and actual economic policy rather than abstract mathematical models—the challenge of Post-Autistic Economics—lies in its demonstration of political economy's complicity with governmentality, a complicity which is hardly unique to the discipline of economics, but which belies claims of neutrality and inserts political economy squarely within the company of other dubious social sciences.

The narrative of nineteenth-century French political economy told in this book points to two fruitful paths for additional research. First, it suggests the need to pursue particular questions and themes into the present. What are the social issues challenging the scientific claims of twenty-first-century French economics? In what way do these new social concerns resemble the nineteenth-century *question sociale*, and by what means is French economics fending off the challenge? In what type of disciplinary gymnastics has contemporary French economics engaged so as to defend itself from the charge of being a dubious science? In what way do those disciplinary gymnastics mirror those of nineteenth-century political economists, with their cautious and complicated distinctions between *économie politique* and *économie sociale,* science and art, pure and applied political economy?

Second, the story I have told here also suggests the need for comparative research. The story of nineteenth-century French political economy—of a self-proclaimed scientific discipline attempting to purge the unanticipated and uncomfortable consequences of industrial development from its disciplinary confines—may well be notable for what it reveals simultaneously about the distinctiveness of the French case, as well as its resemblance to circumstances elsewhere in Europe. For instance, if the tactical considerations that French economists faced during the nineteenth century may have been uniquely French—for instance, the need to voice their jurisdictional claims to the state; the legacy of the French Revolution; the particular structures of higher education which constrained where political economy could have been institutionalized—the processes of disciplinary formation and boundary protection may not have been. Thus, how did the particular developmental trajectory of French political economy compare to disciplinary developments in neighboring nations such as Great Britain, Germany, Italy, or Austria? What did the nineteenth-century histories of political economy in these countries look like? Where did they converge with, and where did they diverge from, the situation in France?

Similarly, the disciplinary challenge facing French political economists during the nineteenth century—to recognize and then manage the unanticipated and deleterious effects of industrial capitalism—must hardly have been peculiar to France. And thus, was the encounter with the unforeseen consequences of industrialization as much of a dilemma in other countries experiencing industrial development as it was in France? Did the British "Condition of England Question" function in the same way for British economists as *la question sociale* did for French economists: as a challenge either to be grafted onto the science of political economy or excluded from it? Was there a German, Italian, Austrian, or Dutch equivalent of the French *question sociale*? Was the French debate part of a broader international discussion, with European equivalents of *économie sociale*? Was the struggle to hide *la question sociale* and move the unforeseen dysfunctions of capitalism out of the discipline of economics into other realms (whether social economy, social work, criminology, psychology, or sociology) uniquely French or not? How did other European economists engage with the unexpected consequences of industrialization?

Comparative work could also explore the contributions of the dubious science of political economy to extra-juridical, extra-governmental regulation—in other words, to governmentality—beyond the French context. Can one find, elsewhere in Europe, the same unintended contribution of political economy to the spread of disciplinary techniques and to governmentality? If the failure to solve *la question sociale* in France, despite almost a century of efforts, nonetheless produced an explosion of information that rendered French workers more visible, better-known, and thus more efficiently governable, did European equivalents of *la question sociale* operate similarly and with similar effects? I have argued that *la question sociale*, besides being an unanticipated and exasperating challenge to the self-identified science of political economy, was an overarching, poorly-defined but easily-identified problem that enabled the collection of information, aided in the creation and protection of academic disciplines that studied this problem, and focused attention on certain people and certain issues, while diverting attention from others. Thus, did *la question sociale* operate in nineteenth-century France the way social problems such as "the problem of the family," "the problem of crime," "the problem of race" or "the problem of immigration" have worked, and continue to work, in contemporary American and European discourse? How do these newer constructions enable the collection of information, the spread of disciplinary techniques, and the creation of academic disciplines? How do they constrain what may or may not be said? And what, finally, do they share with nineteenth-century France's *question sociale*?

If anything, I hope this narrative has demonstrated the significance of using history as an analytical tool in telling the story of academic disciplines. While hardly a new observation, it nonetheless bears repeating, particularly in a narrative of a discipline that continues to cling to claims of certainty, predictability, and measurability. Political economists may have started out wary of history's ambiguity, its ineffectiveness as a source of universal, fixed laws of any type. In their pursuit of status, it was physics and mathematics, not history, upon which nineteenth-century French political economists modeled their discipline. But to their credit, most of them eventually relented, recognizing not simply that they had never strayed far from history, regularly rewriting their past and their "scientific" tenets in order to support their claims to status and institutional power, but also that if political economy was not the certain, exact science they had always hoped it was, perhaps it could aspire to different, but equally significant, objectives than those of physical scientists. By the end of the nineteenth century, whatever political economy had lost in terms of its claims to certainty, truth, and universality, it may well have gained in its ability to prescribe rather than just predict, and to imagine alternatives to the status quo.[5] Behind the façade of science readopted by contemporary economics, behind its claims to be an exact, mathematical science, lies the complicated and ambiguous history of a truly social science, a history of dubiousness but also of a sincere commitment to something more than mathematical models: to people, rather than curves.

Notes

Introduction

1. For an array of thinking on the challenges to neo-classical economics, see Edward Fullbrook, ed., *Real World Economics: A Post-Autistic Economics Reader* (London: Anthem Press, 2006); Peter Monaghan, "Taking on 'Rational Man': Dissident Economists fight for a Niche in the Discipline," *Chronicle of Higher Education* (January 24, 2003), http://chronicle.com/weekly/v49/i20/20a01201.htm; Stanley Alcorn and Ben Solarz, "The Autistic Economist," *Yale Economic Review: A Yale University Student Publication* (Summer 2006), http://www.yaleeconomic review .com/issues/2006_summer/ autistic_economist.html. As a movement that began with students, it is perhaps not surprising that many challengers to orthodox economics have used the Internet as a means of exchanging information; see the websites of the Post-Autistic Economics Network [www.paecon.net], Autisme-Économie [www. autisme-economie.org], and Economía Critica [www.economiacritica. org].
2. "The French Students' Petition," Appendix I, Fullbrook, ed., *Real World Economics,* 471–2.
3. Deborah Campbell, "Kick it Over! The Rise of Post-Autistic Economics," *Adbusters 55* (October 2004), http://adbusters.org/the_magazine/55/Kick_it_Over_The_Rise_ of_ Post-Autistic_Economics.html.
4. Théodore Fix, "De la manière d'observer les faits économiques," *Journal des économistes* [henceforth *JE*] 12 (1845): 98.
5. See Campbell, "Kick it Over!" and Monaghan, "Taking on 'Rational Man.'"
6. The term "dubious science" is Michel Foucault's, who used the term to refer to what is more conventionally labeled the human, or the social, sciences, and to distinguish them from what he labeled the "normal" sciences, such as mathematics, chemistry, and physics. Michel Foucault, "Truth and Power," in Colin Gordon, ed., *Power/ Knowledge: Selected Interviews and Other Writings, 1972-1977* (New York; Pantheon Books, 1980), 109.
7. I have borrowed this phrase from Jan Goldstein's *Console and Classify: The French Psychiatric Profession in the Nineteenth Century* (Cambridge: Cambridge University Press, 1987), 192.
8. Jan Goldstein, "Foucault among the Sociologists: The "Disciplines" and the History of the Professions," *History and Theory*, vol. 23, no. 2 (1984): 175–78.
9. Michel Foucault, *"Society Must Be Defended": Lectures at the Collège de France, 1975-1976*, ed. Mauro Bertani and Alessandro Fontana (New York: Picador, 2003),

7-10. For helpful discussions of genealogy, see John S. Ransom, *Foucault's Discipline: The Politics of Subjectivity* (Durham: Duke University Press, 1997), 78-100; and Hubert L. Dreyfus and Paul Rabinow, *Michel Foucault: Beyond Structuralism and Hermeneutics* (Chicago: The University of Chicago Press, 1982), 104-117.

10. Foucault, *"Society Must Be Defended"*, 10.

11. For the voices of French industrialists and workers, this book relies primarily on archival material pertaining to two of nineteenth-century France's key industrial towns, Mulhouse and Le Creusot, held in the following archival collections: the Archives départementales du Haut-Rhin; the Archives départementales du Saône-et-Loire; the Archives municipales de Mulhouse; the Académie François Bourdon; the Archives de la Société Mulhousienne des cites ouvrières; the Archives des houillères de Blanzy; the Écomusée du Creusot; and the Archives nationales. The industrialists of Mulhouse and Le Creusot also wrote about their paternalist efforts, and their published writings, particularly the *Bulletin de la Société Industrielle de Mulhouse*, provide important material to supplement archival sources.

Chapter One

1. The phrase "the dismal science" was first used by Thomas Carlyle to refer to the British political economy of Thomas Malthus and David Ricardo. According to Roger Backhouse, by the early nineteenth century, "the term 'economist' came to denote someone with an identifiable approach to politics and a congenitally hard heart." Roger E. Backhouse, *The Ordinary Business of Life: A History of Economics from the Ancient World to the Twenty-First Century* (Princeton: Princeton University Press, 2002), 135.

2. Andrew Abbott, *The System of Professions: An Essay on the Division of Expert Labor* (Chicago: The University of Chicago Press, 1988), 8.

3. Ibid., 60.

4. Ibid.

5. For my discussion of the basic tenets of political economy, I am drawing upon Georges Burdeau, *Le libéralisme* (Paris: Éditions Seuil, 1979); William Coleman, *Death is a Social Disease: Public Health and Political Economy in Early Industrial France* (Madison: University of Wisconsin Press, 1982), 59-74; Albert O. Hirschman, *The Passions and the Interests: Political Arguments for Capitalism before its Triumph* (Princeton: Princeton University Press, 1977); Martin S. Staum, "The Institute economists: from Physiocracy to entrepreneurial capitalism," *History of Political Economy* 19, no. 4 (Winter 1987): 525-50; Backhouse, *The Ordinary Business of Life*; Robert L. Heilbroner, *The Worldly Philosophers: The Lives, Times and Ideas of the Great Economic Thinkers* (New York: Simon and Schuster, 1961); and Charles Gide and Charles Rist, *A History of Economic Doctrines from the Time of the Physiocrats to the Present Day*, 7th ed. (Boston: D. C. Heath, 1948).

6. The *Dictionnaire de l'économie politique* defined the task of political economy as the study of the phenomena of production, distribution, and consumption of wealth. Ambroise Clément, "Introduction," *Dictionnaire de l'économie politique*, Charles Coquelin and G.-U. Guillaumin, eds. (Paris: Guillaumin, 1852-3), 1:*x*.
7. Léon Faucher, "Coalition des ouvriers charpentiers," *Journal des économistes* [henceforth *JE*] 12, no. 45 (August 1845): 25-7.
8. William Coleman notes the three legislative steps that legalized the principle of *laissez-faire* in France. The first law made inventions the private property of the inventor. The second abolished the old corporate structure of Ancien Régime France and the corporations that had restricted (in the minds of economists) the liberty of trade. The third was the *loi Le Chapelier* which prevented coalitions between masters or between workers. Coleman, *Death is a Social Disease*, 62.
9. Michel Chevalier, "Du progrès: discours prononcé à l'ouverture de son cours au Collège de France," *JE* 31, no. 129 (January 1852): 29.
10. Ibid., 31. On the other hand, in a statement which suggests the divergences among economists, Charles Dunoyer also asserted that insofar as workers appeared less capable of shouldering self-responsibility, they could effectively be described as being less free than other classes in society. Charles Dunoyer, *L'industrie et la morale considerées dans leurs rapports avec la liberté* (Paris: A. Sautelet, 1825), 393.
11. Charles Dunoyer, "Des objections qu'on a soulevées dans ces derniers temps contre le régime de la concurrence," *JE*, vol. 1 (1841): 134. For further analysis of Dunoyer's emphasis upon self-responsibility, see Edgar Allix, "La déformation de l'économie politique libérale après Jean-Baptiste Say: Charles Dunoyer," *Revue d'histoire des doctrines économiques et sociales*, vol. 4 (1911): 115-47.
12. Frédéric Bastiat, *Harmonies économiques* (Paris: Guillaumin, 1851), 524.
13. Ambroise Clément, "Introduction," *Dictionnaire*, 1:*xi*. According to Clement, one of the problems that might have been avoided had more people understood the principles of political economy was the multiplication of governmental and administrative initiatives in place of individual efforts.
14. Dunoyer, "Des objections qu'on a soulevées," *JE*, vol. 1 (1841); and Adolphe Blanqui, "Des dangers du régime prohibitif et de la nécessité d'y remédier," *JE*, vol. 1 (1841). A simple review of the tables of contents in the first few volumes of the *Journal des économistes* suggests the extent and sincerity of economists' anti-interventionist sentiments. Historian Francis Démier notes that the danger of governmental regulation and state ownership was a principal feature of Blanqui's early work, but—significantly—a feature that would change as Blanqui moved out of the rarefied sphere of abstract economic thought and into daily contact with both the industrial class as well as the working class. Francis Démier, "Adolphe Blanqui, un économiste libéral fâce à la revolution industrielle, 1794-1854," 2 vols., thèse de troisième cycle, Université de Paris X (Nanterre), 1979, ch. 1 and ch. 3.
15. In its most extreme form, this sentiment could be expressed in Charles Dunoyer's fashion: "The height of perfection would be when everyone worked and no one governed." Cited in Allix, "La déformation de l'économie politique libérale après Jean-Baptiste Say," 119.

16. According to Georges Burdeau, this assumption of the fundamental similarity of all individuals' interests suggests the optimism inherent to liberal economics. Were human difference to be inserted into the system, particularly *class* difference, the entire philosophical system would crumble. Burdeau, *Le liberalisme*, 104.
17. Jean-Baptiste Say, *Traité d'économie politique, ou simple exposition de la manière dont se forment, se distribuent, et se consomment les richesses* (Paris: Deterville, 1803), 413.
18. Edgar Allix, "Jean-Baptiste Say et les origines de l'industrialisme," *Revue d'économie politique* 24 (1910): 362.
19. Léon Faucher, "Coalition des ouvriers charpentiers," *JE* 12, no. 45 (August 1845): 25–7.
20. Ibid., 25–33. Strikes and coalitions were prohibited in France by the *loi Le Chapelier*, passed in June of 1791. For more on the *loi Le Chapelier*, see William Coleman, *Death is a Social Disease*, 62–5.
21. Dunoyer, "Des objections qu'on a soulevées," 25.
22. Ibid., 132. Similarly, political economist Théodore Fix wrote in 1842 that "the well-being of the working classes in France is the rule and destitution the exception. This destitution has two causes: the usual and most frequent cause is the debauchery and sloth of the workers. Dissolute living is an individual vice that in no way can be imputed to our social organization." Théodore Fix, "De l'esprit progressif et de l'esprit de conservation en économie politique," *JE* 2 (1842): 222.
23. Coleman, *Death is a Social Disease*, *xv*.
24. For Charles Dunoyer, for instance, the only true remedy for working-class misery was the regime of free trade and free competition. It was free trade and free competition that would create opportunities for workers; that would demonstrate the importance of self-responsibility and all the virtues that accompanied it (for instance, hard work, savings, and morality); and that would demonstrate to workers the possibility of self-improvement open to them. Dunoyer, "Des objections qu'on a soulevées," 12-43, 129-146.
25. Fix, "De l'ésprit progressif et de l'ésprit de conservation en *économie politique*," 254.
26. Joseph Garnier, *Tableau des causes de la misère et des remèdes qu'on peut y apporter* (Paris: Garnier Frères, 1858), 18.
27. Eugène Buret, "De l'exercice de la charité dans les circonstances actuelles," *JE* 2 (1842): 317–35; Horace Say, "De l'administration du département de la Seine et de la ville de Paris," *JE* 10 (1845): 124–48.
28. Historians of economic thought have been careful to note that Adam Smith's ideas were far from original, but were borrowed from David Hume, William Petty, John Law, John Locke, Bernard Mandeville, François Quesnay, and David Hume.
29. In his 1803 *Traité d'économie politique*, Jean-Baptiste Say himself described the *Wealth of Nations*: "The work of Smith is but a confusing assemblage of the soundest principles of political economy, backed up by lucid examples and the strangest statistical notions, mixed with instructive reflections, but it is neither a complete treatise of the one or of the other; his book is a vaste chaos of sound ideas, jumbled with positive knowledge." Originally cited in Lucette Le Van-Lemesle, *Le Juste ou le*

Riche: L'enseignement de l'économie politique 1815-1950 (Paris: Comité pour l'histoire économique et financière de la France, 2004), 27.

30. Charles Coquelin, "Économie politique," *Dictionnaire,* 1:644. This assessment seems not to have altered by 1911, when Edgar Allix argued that Say had always treated political economy as a concrete, objective science akin to physics, rather than an art. Edgar Allix, "La méthode et la conception de l'économie politique dans l'oeuvre de Jean-Baptiste Say," *Revue d'histoire des doctrines économiques et sociales* 4 (1911): 321-60.

31. Backhouse, *The Ordinary Business of Life,* 137. For a discussion of the clear principles that Say substituted for Smith's hodgepodge of details, see Emma Rothschild, *Economic Sentiments: Adam Smith, Condorcet, and the Enlightenment* (Cambridge: Harvard University Press, 2001), 237.

32. Joyce Appleby, Lynn Hunt, Margaret Jacob, *Telling the Truth About History* (New York: W.W. Norton, 1994), 15.

33. The apparent heroism of political economy would only have been reinforced by the repression that French economists often suffered. The Restoration regime placed the courses of Charles Comte, Charles Dunoyer, and Adolphe Blanqui under police surveillance. Comte was himself regularly tailed by the police. An economist as well-known as Say, whose courses were also attended, not just by legitimate students, but by police spies, was forced to read all his lectures, avoid all spontaneous lecturing, and answer students' questions only when they arrived by personal letter. For the surveillance of economists under the Restoration, see Le Van-Lemesle, *Le Juste ou le Riche,* 69 and 83.

34. In an 1820 letter that Say wrote to Thomas Malthus, he wrote "He [the economist] must be content to remain an impartial spectator. What we owe to the public is to tell them how and why such-and-such a fact is the consequence of another. Whether the conclusion be welcomed or rejected, it is enough that the economist should have demonstrated its cause; but he must give no advice." Originally cited in Gide and Rist, *A History of Economic Doctrines,* 125-6.

35. Cited in Allix, "La méthode et la conception de l'économie politique," 353-54.

36. Adam Smith, *An Inquiry into the Nature and Causes of the Wealth of Nations,* Edwin Cannan, ed. (New York: The Modern Library, 1937), 734. For a discussion of Smith's understanding of the necessity of government intervention, see Heilbroner, *The Worldly Philosophers,* 52-4.

37. Backhouse, *The Ordinary Business of Life,* 127-28.

38. Ibid., 128-29.

39. Smith, *The Wealth of Nations,* 460.

40. Ibid., 66.

41. Ibid. Smith also recognized that employers had the advantage when it came to coalitions. Coalitions of employers were easier to organize than those of workers since there were fewer employers. The law prohibited coalitions of workers, but did not prohibit those of employers (although they were never authorized). Even more unfairly, the public was regularly informed about workers' coalitions, but seldom

about employers'. As a result, the public often erroneously concluded that employers' coalitions did not exist.

42. Rothschild, *Economic Sentiments*, 2.

43. Richard Whatmore, *Republicanism and the French Revolution: An Intellectual History of Jean-Baptiste Say's Political Economy* (Oxford: Oxford University Press, 2000), 4–5.

44. According to Whatmore, "...a straightforwardly 'liberal' Smith can be found neither in Say's writings nor in those of any other political economist. If Smith was used to support a variety of political standpoints in the 1790s, how did Say come to form his opinion of Smith? This was the question which none of Say's family addressed, preferring to sketch an idealized growth of what was already deemed to be the most successful science of society." Ibid., 9.

45. Ibid., 6.

46. Ibid., 17–33.

47. Ibid., 129.

48. Ibid., 124. Whatmore is quoting from Say's article "Boniface Véridick à Polyscope, sur son projet de theater pour le people," *La Décade philosophique, littéraire et politique, par une société de républicains* 10 (10 Germinal, an IV): 38–44.

49. Whatmore, *Republicanism and the French Revolution*, 157.

50. Ibid., 146.

51. Ibid., 177–83. Like Smith, Say presumed a certain social and legal structure necessary for the proper working of the laws of political economy. First and foremost, government was responsible for assuring the security of private property, including the legal protection of labor, also a source of private property. Government was also responsible for general defense. Like Smith, Say believed that government had an interest in providing goods "beyond the means of private capital," for instance, roads, canals, bridges, and public education, and recognized that government intervention was necessary when public safety demanded it, as in times of scarcity, when the grain trade could not be left unregulated for fear of public uprisings.

52. Ibid.,167. According to Whatmore, Say used the terms "self-interest" and "enlightened self-interest" interchangeably. If he believed that "self-interest [was] the driving force of modern society," it was a self-interest that was "informed, independent, and the product of reflection." Self-interest for Say, then, did not mean *selfishness*; it did not mean indifference or callousness toward others.

53. Ibid., 217.

54. Rothschild, *Economic Sentiments*, 30.

55. Ibid., 48.

56. Ibid., 247.

57. Ibid., 58. Rothschild argues that the divorcing of political freedom from economic freedom, something that Smith himself could not have imagined, was first accomplished by Smith's biographer, Dugald Stewart, writing in 1793: "Stewart's account suggested that there were two spheres of life, the commercial and the political. Political economy was concerned with commercial or economic life....'Political freedom,' by contrast, was an attribute of political life, and was outside

the scope of political economy." Rothschild, *Economic Sentiments*, 59–61. I have borrowed Rothschild's phrase "a retiring, innocuous sort of person," which she uses to characterize (and ridicule) the disposition given by Dugald Stewart to the fictional Adam Smith.

58. This would not be the only time that historical context would entail a particular reading of Jean-Baptiste Say's ideas. In the 1860s, French economists were anxious to form alliances with the imperial state that would result in the solidification of the discipline of political economy. In a biographical essay on Say for the *Dictionnaire de l'économie politique*, Ambroise Clément played down Say's anti-clericalism and anti-Bonapartism; uncoupled political liberalism from economic liberalism; and minimized the inspiration of the French Revolution in Say's work. To portray Say as a republican, and thus political economy as a revolutionary discipline, potentially subversive of an authoritarian, imperial state, was, in the 1860s, to undermine economists' efforts at self-promotion. For Le Van-Lemesle's discussion of this rewriting of Say's biography, see Le Van-Lemesle, *Le Juste ou le Riche*, 25–45.
59. Whatmore, *Republicanism and the French Revolution*, 9.
60. Edgar Allix, "La deformation de l'économie politique," 116.
61. I have used a wide variety of sources for these biographical sketches. For biographical details on Charles Dunoyer, see Allix, "La deformation de l'économie politique," 115–47. Also "Charles Dunoyer," *Nouvelle Biographie Génerale* (Paris: Firmin-Didot Frères, 1857). For Théodore Fix and Joseph Garnier, see "Théodore Fix" and "Joseph Garnier," *Nouvelle Biographie Générale*. For Frédéric Bastiat, see "Frédéric Bastiat," *Nouvelle Biographie Générale*; "Chronique" *JE*, vol. 15, no. 57 (Aug. 1846): 101–4. For Louis-René Villermé, see Coleman, *Death is a Social Disease*. For Louis Reybaud, see "Louis Reybaud," *Nouvelle Biographie Générale*; and "Chronique" *JE*, vol. 15, no. 57 (Aug. 1846): 101–4; *Dictionnaire d'économie politique*. For Adolphe Blanqui, see Démier, "Adolphe Blanqui, un économiste libérale"; and Claudine Fontanon and André Grelon, eds., *Les Professeurs du Conservatoire National des Arts et Métiers: Dictionnaire biographique, 1794–1955*, vol. 1 (Paris: Institut national de recherché pédagogique, 1994), 185–94. For Henri Baudrillard, see "Henri Baudrillard," *Nouvelle Biographie Générale*. For Gilbert-Urbain Guillaumin, see Lucette Le Van-Lemesle, "Guillaumin, Éditeur d'économie politique, 1801–64," *Revue d'économie politique*, no. 2 (1985): 134–49; and Le Van-Lemesle, *Le Juste ou le Riche*, 102–15. And finally, for Louis Wolowski, see Fontanon and Grelon, eds., *Les Professeurs du Conservatoire National des Arts et Métiers*, 2:677–87.
62. Guillaumin, for instance, has been described by historian Lucette Le Van-Lemesle as remaining a confirmed republican throughout his life. Louis Reybaud has also been described as holding republican sentiments until 1848, when the events of both February and June "opened his eyes." "Louis Reybaud," *Nouvelle Biographie Générale*.
63. Along with Louis Reybaud, for whom 1848 seems to have been a momentous date, Henri Baudrillart, who would become Michel Chevalier's successor to the chair of political economy at the Collège de France in 1850, was also attracted to political economy in 1848. "Henri Baudrillart," *Nouvelle Biographie Générale*.

64. The first political economist of any renown whose professional biography looks at all familiar from a contemporary point-of-view was Émile Levasseur, who held chairs of political economy at both the *Collège de France* and the *Conservatoire des arts et métiers* under the Third Republic. But even Levasseur, who obtained his *licence ès letters* in 1850 and spent fifteen years teaching at a secondary school level, was trained *not* as an economist, but rather as an historian and geographer. Fontanon and Grelon, eds., *Les Professeurs du Conservatoire National des Arts et Métiers,* 2:105–6.
65. Théodore Fix, for instance, won a prize in 1840 for his work on customs; later in the century, Émile Levasseur also won a variety of prizes from the Academy. "Théodore Fix," *Nouveau Biographie Générale*; and Fontanon and Grelon, eds., *Les Professeurs du Conservatoire National des Arts et Métiers,* 2:107.
66. Ibid., 2:677–87.
67. "Chronique," *JE,* 15, no. 57 (Aug. 1846): 101–4.
68. Charles Gide, "The Economic Schools and the Teaching of Political Economy in France," *Political Science Quarterly* 5, no. 4 (1890): 603–35.
69. Yves Breton, "Les économistes, le pouvoir politique et l'ordre social en France entre 1830 et 1851," *Histoire, Économie, et Société,* no. 2 (1985): 233–252.
70. Madeleine Ventre-Denis, "Sciences sociales et Université au XIXe siècle: Une tentative d'enseignement de l'économie politique à Paris sous la Restauration," *Revue historique* 520 (1976): 336. Ventre-Denis is here quoting Charles Comte.
71. Breton, "Les économistes," 233–252. Émile Levasseur, in his 1901 article on the *Conservatoire,* also mentions that Adolphe Blanqui was much disliked by protectionists in the Chamber of Deputies under the July Monarchy. Émile Levasseur, *L'enseignement de l'économie politique au Conservatoire des arts et métiers* (Paris: A. Chevalier-Marescq et Compagnie, 1901), 8.
72. Lucette Le Van-Lemesle, "La promotion de l'économie politique en France au dix-neuvième siècle jusqu'à son introduction dans les facultés, 1815-1881," *Revue d'histoire moderne et contemporaine* 27 (April-June 1980): 280.
73. These were the words originally used by the government minister Élie Decazes who oversaw the project of transformation. Cited in Le Van-Lemesle, "La promotion de l'économie politique," 276.
74. Le Van-Lemesle, "La promotion de l'économie politique," 276, 285; George Weisz, *The Emergence of Modern Universities in France, 1863-1914* (Princeton: Princeton University Press, 1983), 18–19.
75. Fontanon and Grelon, eds., *Les Professeurs du Conservatoire national des arts et métiers,* 1:27.
76. Ibid., 1:18.
77. Ibid., 1:29. The *Conservatoire*'s typical students could, of course, only attend courses during the evening. It is for this reason that the Restoration Minister Villèle's demand that courses be shifted from evenings to afternoons emptied many courses of much of their audience. When courses resumed in the evenings in 1829, attendance again rose.
78. Ibid. For Blanqui's success at the *Conservatoire,* see Demier, "Adolphe Blanqui, un économiste libérale," ch. 3.

79. Originally cited in Joseph Garnier, *De l'origine et de la filation du mot économie politique et des divers autres noms donnés à la science économique* (Paris: Guillaumin, 1852), 25.
80. Ibid.
81. Le Van-Lemesle, "La promotion de l'économie politique," 279–80.
82. Le Van-Lemesle, *Le Juste ou le Riche*, 81.
83. For more on the *Académie*, see William Coleman, *Death is a Social Disease*, 7–8; as well as Francis Demier, "Adolphe Blanqui, un économiste libérale," ch. 3.
84. Le Van-Lemesle, "La promotion de l'économie politique en France," 282.
85. Le Van-Lemesle, *Le Juste ou le Riche*, 102. For my discussion of Guillaumin's contributions to French political economy, I have relied upon Le Van-Lemesle, *Le Juste ou le Riche*, as well as her earlier article, "Guillaumin, Éditeur d'économie politique, 1801-64."
86. For a brief history of the *Société des Économistes* see the first volume of the *Annales de la Société d'économie politique*, published for the first time in 1846 by *Guillaumin et Compagnie*. Also see Le Van-Lemesle, *Le Juste ou le Riche*, 139–45. It is Le Van-Lemesle who "names" Pierre Bos.
87. Le Van-Lemesle, "La promotion de l'économie politique en France," 284-85. According to Le Van-Lemesle, membership continued to increase: in 1849 to 80 members; in 1859 to 117; in 1864 to 165; and in 1874 to 211. Le Van-Lemesle, *Le Juste ou le Riche*, 142.
88. Démier describes the *Société* as having been characterized by its openness and its free-for-all nature, but also by its elitism and its lack of contact with real, ground-level economic activity. Démier, "Adolphe Blanqui, un économiste libérale," 400.
89. The first issue of the *Journal des économistes* was published on December 15, 1841; its last issue was published in December of 1939.
90. In his introductory essay to the first volume, Louis Reybaud noted this goal of publicity, pointing out that an economic journal would challenge those who accused political economy of not caring about human beings. Louis Reybaud, "Introduction," *JE* 1 (1841): 2.
91. For my discussion of the *Journal des économistes* I have relied upon Le Van-Lemesle, *Le Juste ou le Riche*; Le Van-Lemesle, "La promotion de l'économie politique en France;" Michel Lutfalla, "Aux origines du libéralisme économique en France: le *Journal des économistes*, analyse du contenu de la première série, 1841-1853," *Revue d'histoire économique et sociale* 4 (1972): 494–517; and Luc Marco and Evelyne Laurent, *Le Journal des économistes, 1841–1940* (Paris: Éditions de l'Association Nationale des Docteur ès Sciences Economiques, 1990).
92. The distinctiveness of the *Journal des économistes* is particularly noticeable when compared to another journal, *L'économiste français*, founded in 1873 and edited by Paul Leroy-Beaulieu. Whereas the goal of the *Journal des économistes* was to provide scientific analysis of the economy to non-specialists, the goal of Leroy-Beaulieu's journal was to provide practical information to businessmen. According to historian Lucette Le Van-Lemesle, the *Journal des économistes* was thus a profoundly revolutionary publication, aimed at radically changing the *status quo* along the lines of

liberal theory, whereas *L'économiste français* was a profoundly conservative one, aimed at providing the type of information that would make a few people—namely its readers—rich. Le Van-Lemesle, *Le Juste ou le Riche*, 363–73.

93. Jean-Baptiste Say, "Lettre inedite sur l'utilité d'établir l'enseignment de l'économie politique dans les écoles industrielles," *JE* 13, no. 53 (April 1846): 259. The letter has also been reproduced in its entirety as Appendix 2 in Le Van-Lemesle, *Le Juste ou le Riche*, 713–17.
94. Reybaud, "Introduction," *JE* 1 (1841): 1.
95. Lutfalla, "Aux origines du libéralisme économique en France," 498. Lutfalla also quotes economist Joseph Garnier who argued in 1845 that for too long "the monopoly of public administration has been left to short-sighted men," a situation that the *Journal des économistes* would fix. Lutfalla, "Aux origines du libéralisme économique en France," 499.
96. Hippolyte Dussard, "Chronique," *JE*, vol. 5 (1843): 127.
97. F. de la Farelle, "De la nécessité de fonder en France l'enseignement de l'économie politique," *JE*, vol. 14, no. 53 (1845): 97–105. Also see the "Chronique," *JE*, vol. 11, no. 41 (April 1845): 109–12.
98. Farelle, "De la nécessité de fonder," 102–4; Blaise, "De l'enseignement de l'économie politique en France," 52.
99. Coleman, *Death is a Social Disease*, 219.
100. For more on Social Catholicism see Katherine A. Lynch, *Family, Class, and Ideology in Early Industrial France: Social Policy and the Working-Class Family, 1825–1848* (Madison: University of Wisconsin Press, 1988), 31–64.
101. Jerome-Adolphe Blanqui, friend and protégé of Jean-Baptiste Say, professor at both the *École spéciale du commerce* and the *Conservatoire des arts et métiers*, is an important case in point. According to his biographer Francis Démier, Blanqui's post at the *Conservatoire* moved him out of the rarefied atmosphere of scientific discourse and into the real world of the working class. And as a result, his *laissez-faire* convictions gradually began to evolve. Démier, "Adolphe Blanqui, un économiste libéral," 426.

Chapter Two

1. Louis Reybaud, "Introduction," *Journal des économistes* [henceforth *JE*] 1 (1841): 2.
2. Ibid., 3.
3. Reybaud pointed out that while medicine had not yet cured all illnesses, nor philosophy solved the problem of existence, neither science was any less valuable or important for its failure. Ibid., 9.
4. Ibid., 6.
5. Ibid., 10. Reybaud asserted that the creation of a *Revue de l'Économie politique* would be one answer to those who accused political economy of not caring about human beings.
6. Ibid., 9-10.

7. Giovanna Procacci, "Governing Poverty: Sources of the Social Question in Nineteenth-Century France," in Jan Goldstein, ed., *Foucault and the Writing of History* (Cambridge: Basil Blackwell Ltd., 1994), 211.
8. The following is a mere sample of the wide variety of historical scholarship that has contributed to the topic of *la question sociale*: Louis Chevalier, *Classes laborieuses et classes dangereuses à Paris pendant la première moitié du dix-neuvième siècle* (Paris: Hachette, 1978); William Coleman, *Death is a Social Disease: Public Health and Political Economy in Early Industrial France* (Madison: University of Wisconsin Press, 1982); Jacques Donzelot, *The Policing of Families* (New York: Random House, 1979); François Ewald, *L'État providence* (Paris: Éditions Grasset, 1986); Katherine A. Lynch, *Family, Class, and Ideology in Early Industrial France: Social Policy and the Working-Class Family, 1825–1848* (Madison: University of Wisconsin Press, 1988); Giovanna Procacci, *Gouverner la Misère: la Question Sociale en France, 1789–1848* (Paris: Éditions Seuil, 1993); Joan Scott, "'L'ouvrière! Mot impie, sordide...': Women Workers in the Discourse of French Political Economy, 1840-1860," *Gender and the Politics of History* (New York: Columbia University Press, 1988).
9. Procacci, *Gouverner la Misère*, 13.
10. Janet R. Horne, *A Social Laboratory for Modern France: the Musée Social and the Rise of the Welfare State* (Durham: Duke University Press, 2002), 24.
11. *Rapport de la Commission d'examen des produits industriels de Saône-et-Loire, sur l'Établissement du Creuzot* (Mâcon: Imprimerie de Dejuissieu, 1849), 11-12.
12. See Alain Cottereau, "Les règlements d'atelier au cours de la Révolution Industrielle en France," in *Les Règlements d'ateliers, 1798–1936*, Anne Biroleau, ed. (Paris: Bibliothèque Nationale, 1984), for an excellent overview of these factory regulations. For one such *règlement d'atelier*, see Article 20 of the Schneider steel factories' *Règlement Général* of 1900 listed in *Économie sociale: Institutions de MM. Schneider et Compagnie* (Nevers: Imprimerie Mazeron Frères, 1905), 5–6.
13. "Rapport de la Commission chargée d'examiner les mémoires pour le prix traitant de l'industrialisme, dans ses rapports avec la société, sous le point de vue moral, lu par le M. le docteur Weber," *Bulletin de la Société Industrielle de Mulhouse* [henceforth *BSIM*] 12, Bulletin 59 (1839): 415–16.
14. Daniel Le Grand, *Lettre d'un industriel des montagnes des Vosges* (Paris: F.G. Levrault, 1838), 19. Le Grand wrote that before 1830 he had never been concerned with publicly expressing his views on the working class, but that the events of the July Revolution had encouraged him to take up a pen in protest.
15. See the collection of letters between departmental officials, dating from 1827 to 1870, in the Archives Départementales du Haut-Rhin [ADHR] 1/Z/513. Also, André Koechlin to the Prefect of the Haut-Rhin, 23 December 1831, Archives Municipales de Mulhouse [AMM] J/II/Hf1.
16. Hartmann et Compagnie, Malmerspach, to the Juge de Paix of St.-Amarin, 27 May 1853, ADHR 10/M/9.

17. "Demande à la Chambre de Pairs et à la Chambre des Deputés de la suppression des bureaux de loterie dans les villes exclusivement manufacturières," *BSIM* 1, Bulletin 4 (1828): 273–74.
18. Le Grand, *Lettre d'un industriel*, 14–15.
19. "Rapport de la Commission," *BSIM* 12, Bulletin 59 (1839): 408. For a more extensive and in-depth analysis of the problems of abandoned children and parental exploitation, see Katherine A. Lynch's *Family, Class and Ideology in Early Industrial France*, chs. 4–5.
20. "Rapport de la Commission," *BSIM* 12, Bulletin 59 (1839): 409.
21. The best example of this negative portrayal of working-class women can be found in Louis-René Villermé's *Tableau de l'état physique et moral des ouvriers.* Here Villermé described women who gave their children a crude sleeping medicine as evidence that alcohol use had become a standard practice among workers. The largest amount of medicine, he argued, was purchased on Sundays, Mondays and holidays, days, in other words, when these women spent their time in *cafés* and left their children at home unattended. Louis-René Villermé, *Tableau de l'état physique et moral des ouvriers employés dans les manufactures de coton, de laine et de soie* (Paris: Jules Renouard, 1840), 1:106–7.
22. *Enquête décennale sur les institutions d'initiative privée destinées à favoriser l'amélioration de l'état matériel et moral de la population de la Haute-Alsace: Rapport présenté à la Société industrielle par son comité d'utilité publique à l'occasion de l'Exposition Universelle de 1878* (Mulhouse: Imprimerie de Veuve Bader, 1878), 199–200.
23. Dr. Penot, "Rapport sur la nécéssité d'interdire le travail de nuit dans les manufactures," *BSIM* 24, Bulletin 116 (1852): 89.
24. Eugène Buret, "De l'exercise de la charité dans les circonstances actuelles," *JE* 2 (1842): 332.
25. "Demande à la Chambre de pairs et à la Chambre des Députés de la suppression des bureaux de loterie dans les villes exclusivement manufacturières," *BSIM* 4 (1828), 275; Enquete de 1848–1849 sur le travail, ADHR 10/M/6.
26. Mayor of Mulhouse to the Prefect of the Haut-Rhin, 23 February 1829, ADHR 1/M/69.
27. The basic history of the workers' housing projects in Mulhouse can be found in Achille Penot's article "Project d'habitations pour les classes ouvrières," *BSIM* 24 (June 1852); also see Stephan Jonas, Philippe Heckner and Jean-Michel Knorr, *La cité de Mulhouse (1853–1870): un modèle d'habitat économique et social du dix-neuvième siècle* (Strasbourg: Association de recherche près l'unité pédagogique d'architecture de Strasbourg, 1981). For housing in Montceau-les-Mines, see Amedée Burat, *Société des Houillères de Blanzy: situation de ses établissements en 1877* (Paris: J. Baudry, 1878); and Amedée Burat, *Notice sur les institutions ouvrières des mines de Blanzy* (Dijon: Imprimerie de l'Union Typographique, 1893). Discussion of housing in Le Creusot can be found in Christian Devillers and Bernard Huet, *Le Creusot: Naissance et développement d'une ville industrielle* (Seyssel: Champ Vallon,

1981); and Jean-Pierre Frey, *La ville industrielle et ses urbanités: la distinction ouvrier-employé. Le Creusot, 1870–1930* (Bruxelles: P. Mardaga, 1986).

28. For the history of education in Le Creusot, see Félix Courtois, *Les écoles du Creusot, 1787-1882* (Autun: Imprimerie Dejussieu, 1893); and Jean Forest, *L'emprise* (Paris: La pensée universelle, 1971). See descriptions of the Schneiders' elaborate educational system in *Économie Sociale: institutions de MM. Schneider et Compagnie* and *Les Établissements Schneider: Économie Sociale* (Paris: Imprimerie Générale Lahure, 1912). For Montceau-les-Mines, see Burat, *Société des houillères de Blanzy*, 125; and Jules Chagot, *Note sur les houillères de Blanzy et sur les institutions spéciales pour développer le bien-être matériel et moral des ouvriers* (Paris: Imprimerie de Guyot et Scribe, 1867). For Mulhouse, see *Rapport, fait au nom de la Commission chargée par l'assemblée générale des fabricants du canton de Mulhouse, de présenter un projet sur les moyens à employer pour faire jouir du bienfait de l'instruction primaire les enfants qui peuplent les filateurs et les fabriques*, 11 January 1826, AMM R/I/Cb2.

29. In Le Creusot, for example, the first company infirmary and pharmacy were built in 1837, as soon as the Schneider brothers took over the firm. Two hospitals were built, the first in 1879 and the second in 1894. For women's health care in Montceau-les-Mines, see Société Anonyme des Mines de Houille de Blanzy, *Hôpital des blessés, consultation des nourrissons et goutte de lait; oeuvre du trousseau dans les écoles de filles* (Montceau: Rajaud Frères, 1910).

30. For discussions of *caisses* in Mulhouse, Le Creusot and Montceau-les-Mines, see Denise Herrenschmidt, "Les caisses de secours entre ouvriers à Mulhouse de 1800 à 1870," *Bulletin du Musée historique de Mulhouse* 66 (1958): 69–113; "Règlement de la caisse de secours et des écoles," 1 January 1837, Académie François Bourdon [AFB] DH/0009; and Chagot, *Note sur les houillères de Blanzy.*

31. The first *École ménagère*, or housekeeping school, was organized in Le Creusot in 1906 and was designed to contribute to the amelioration of the well-being of working-class families. The company argued that this well-being was not only dependent upon the work of men within the factory, but equally upon the work of women within the home. "Cahier scolaire de Jeanne Rey," 1912, Ecomusée du Creusot [EC] A/357; also *Les Établissements Schneider: Économie sociale*, 68–69.

32. Gardening was the earliest, and would remain the most important, form of leisure, but by the end of the nineteenth century, firms were also organizing a variety of sports programs, musical groups, and literary groups. For information on workers' gardens see Achille Penot, *Les cités ouvrières de Mulhouse et du département du Haut-Rhin* (Mulhouse: Imprimerie de L.L. Bader, 1867), 80–81; and "Projet de jardins ouvriers," 18 September 1919, EC A/271. For information on other leisure-time activities organized for workers, see "Construction de logements ouvriers," 6 November 1918, AFB SS/420; Burat, *Société des houillères de Blanzy*, p. 126; Chagot, *Note sur les houillères de Blanzy.*

33. Alain Dewerpe, *Le monde du travail en France, 1800–1950* (Paris: Armand Colin, 1989), 79.

34. Public interest in paternalism is demonstrated by the number of inquiries received by the Industrial Society of Mulhouse concerning the *cités ouvrières,* or workers' cities, built by Mulhousian textile manufacturers. By 1865, the Société had received so many requests for information that it decided to print and send brochures in response to these requests. *BSIM* 35 (January 1865).
35. Quoted in the *Centenaire de la Société Industrielle de Mulhouse, 1826–1926,* 2 vols. (Mulhouse: Braun et Compagnie, 1926), 1:97.
36. Assemblée Générale du 25 janvier 1854 and Assemblée Générale du 14 janvier 1861, Archives Nationales [AN] 94/AQ/2-6. See also Rapport du Conseil de Surveillance, 14 January 1863, AN 94/AQ/2-6.
37. "Notice sur la population ouvrière du Creusot," n.d., AFB DH/0010. This undated document appears to be a restatement of a report given by an unnamed member of the Schneider firm to the Chamber of Deputies. The document looks as if it had been cut out of a journal, perhaps the *Journal officiel,* and glued onto separate pages to form a small brochure.
38. "Rapport du gérant," 30 November 1863, AN 187/AQ/3.
39. "Rapport annuel fait à l'assemblée générale par M. Jean Zuber, fils," *BSIM* 2, Bulletin 8 (1829): 235–47.
40. Charles Grad, *Études statistiques sur l'industrie de l'Alsace* (Strasbourg: Librairie Noiriel, 1897), 2:385–89.
41. M. Hartmann-Leibach to the Juge de Paix of St.-Amarin, 23 June 1853, ADHR 10/M/9.
42. "Rapport par Emile Béres sur les causes du malaise industriel et commercial de la France et moyens d'y rémédier," *BSIM* 6, Bulletin 26 (1833): 16.
43. "Rapport de la commission," *BSIM* 12, Bulletin 59 (1839): 394.
44. See, for example, ADHR 10/M/7, which contains letter after letter describing the miseries caused by economic crises in Mulhouse.
45. Louis Reybaud, *Rapport sur la condition morale, intellectuelle et matérielle des ouvriers qui vivent de l'industrie de la laine* (Paris: Didot Frères, 1865), 131.
46. John S. Ransom, *Foucault's Discipline: The Politics of Subjectivity* (Durham: Duke University Press, 1997), 23.
47. For my discussions of the disciplinary technologies of objectification and subjectification, I am relying upon Hubert L. Dreyfus and Paul Rabinow, *Michel Foucault: Beyond Structuralism and Hermeneutics* (Chicago: The University of Chicago Press, 1982), chs. 7–8; Jan Goldstein, "Foucault among the Sociologists: The "Disciplines" and the History of the Professions," *History and Theory* 23, no. 2 (1984); and Ransom, *Foucault's Discipline,* ch. 2.
48. Dreyfus and Rabinow, *Michel Foucault,* 153–8.
49. Ransom, *Foucault's Discipline,* 35.
50. "Prix Salathé," Société Mulhousienne des Cités Ouvrières [SOMCO], Centre Rhénan d'Archives et de Recherches Économiques, Mulhouse, A/1425; Penot, *Les cités ouvrières de Mulhouse,* Appendix 3.
51. *Économie Sociale: institutions de MM. Schneider et Compagnie,* 142. The Établissements Schneider boasted in 1905 that one-quarter of its workforce had been

employed at the forge for more than 25 years, and that it was not at all rare to find families in which eight or more members were employed by the firm, and whose members had been employed for two or three generations.

52. Ewald, *L'État providence*, 122–30.
53. Forest, *L'emprise*, 157. Throughout his memoir, Forest describes his father's slow but steady climb up the employment ladder provided by the Schneiders. He makes it clear, however, that his father's climb depended upon behavior deemed acceptable by the firm. In 1919, for instance, his father was warned that his promotion to *contremaître* would be scuttled unless he got rid of the local café he owned.
54. M. Creteil to the Prefect of the Haut-Rhin, 5 October 1863, ADHR 1/T/548.
55. Achille Penot, "Rapport du comité d'économie sociale sur la construction d'une cité ouvrière à Mulhouse," *BSIM* 25 (1853). Also Mines de Blanzy, *Règlement sur les logements d'employés et d'ouvriers* (Le Creusot, Imprimerie de A. Temporal, 1871).
56. Mines de Blanzy, *Règlement sur les logements d'employés et d'ouvriers.*
57. AFB Register 01L018.
58. Industrialists regularly noted the need for surveillance of cafés, and just as regularly shut them down. Prefect of the Haut-Rhin to the Minister of the Interior, 4 February 1854, ADHR 1/M/66. Also see Forest, *L'emprise* for a discussion of industrial firms' surveillance of local bars. For industrialists' assessment of the dangers of crowded working-class housing, see Achille Penot, "Des institutions de prevoyance fondées par les industriels du Haut-Rhin en faveur de leurs ouvriers," *BSIM* 26, Bulletin 131 (August 1854–July 1855): 411.
59. Alfred de Glehn, "Note sur les logements ouvriers," *BSIM* (June 1907): 258–67.
60. Penot, "Des institutions de prevoyance fondées par les industriels du Haut-Rhin," 412–13.
61. For a variety of workers' testimonials about the benefits of gardens, see the Congrès Regional des Oeuvres d'Assistance, de Prévoyance, et d'Assurance Sociales, *Congrès des oeuvres sociales* (Lille: n.p., 1910), 766. It seems likely, however, that many of these testimonials may reveal more about what industrialists hoped gardens would accomplish than about what workers actually thought.
62. "Coalition d'ouvriers dans l'usine de M. Isaac Koechlin," August 1852, AN BB/30/404 (P753).
63. "Construction de logements ouvriers," 6 Novembre 1918, AFB SS/420. In this report, the author mentioned that one of the aims of the Établissements Schneider was to encourage workers to respect and feel proud of the significant role they played in society. One can assume, however, that the hope that workers would feel proud of their role in society was tied up with the hope that proud workers would be politically conservative workers, and that no worker who considered his or her self-interest to rest with the status quo would be willing to undermine it.
64. Chagot, *Note sur les houillères de Blanzy*, 16.
65. Lynch, *Family, Class and Ideology in Early Industrial France*, 7. Here Lynch draws attention to "the truly innovative character of a point of view that held that the problems of working-class families could be resolved in large part by workers' adoption of personal values and behavior identified with the bourgeoisie."

66. See, for instance, Jean Dollfus, *Note sur les cités ouvrières* (Paris, Imprimerie de E., n.d.); *Centenaire de la Société Industrielle de Mulhouse, 1826–1926*; Penot, *Les cités ouvrières de Mulhouse*; Chagot, *Note sur les houillères de Blanzy*; and *Économie Sociale: Institutions de MM. Schneider et Compagnie.*
67. Théodore Fix, "Situation des classes ouvrières," *JE* 10, no. 37 (Dec. 1844): 30.
68. Rapet, "Des conditions du bien-être pour les classes laborieuses et de l'influence qu'il exerce sur la moralité," *JE* 27, no. 116 (Nov. 1850): 334.
69. Fix, "Situation des classes ouvrières," 28.
70. Louis Reybaud, "La condition morale, intellectuelle et matérielle des ouvriers qui vivent de l'industrie du coton," *JE*, 2d ser., 39, no. 4 (April 1861): 15.
71. Henri Baudrillart, *Des rapports de la morale et de l'économie politique: cours professé au Collège de France* (Paris: Guillaumin, 1860), 565.
72. Villermé, *Tableau,* 2:58.
73. Frédéric Passy, "La famille et la société," *JE*, 2d ser., 30, no. 31 (July 1856): 59–83.
74. Jerome Adolphe Blanqui, "Notice sur la vie et les travaux d'Adam Smith," *JE* 3 (1842): 395. Four years earlier, in 1838, Blanqui had already written that "the time has perhaps come to ask whether the manufacturing system really is an instrument of general prosperity." Jerome Adolphe Blanqui, *Cours d'économie industrielle, 1838–1839* (Paris: J. Angé, 1839), 56.
75. Villermé, *Tableau,* 2:351.
76. Théodore Fix, "Observations sur l'état des classes ouvrières," *JE* 12, no. 48 (1845): 294. Fix argued that because workers were forced to sell their labor power, they were naturally subject to overwork, less-than-perfect working conditions, corrupting influences, and the impossibility of acquiring an education. All these were conditions inherent to being a worker, and conditions that often led to misery, rendering the condition of being a worker inherently dangerous.
77. Henri Baudrillart, "Où en est l'économie politique," *JE*, 2d ser., 41 (1864): 33–34.
78. Antoine Cherbuliez, "Paupérisme," *Dictionnaire de l'économie politique*, Charles Coquelin and G.-U. Guillaumin, eds. (Paris: Guillaumin, 1852–53), 2:337.
79. While Foucault used the terms "governmentality" and "bio-power" as essentially synonymous, for the purposes of clarity I will use the term "governmentality." For my discussions of governmentality I have relied upon Ransom, *Foucault's Discipline*, ch.3; and Dreyfus and Rabinow, *Michel Foucault*, ch. 6.
80. In Foucault's work, the duo power/knowledge refers to the modern relationship between power and knowledge, in which power and knowledge imply one another rather than oppose each other, with power always existing in a relationship with knowledge, and knowledge in a relationship with power. Knowledge is always already an expression of power, and power as it is exercised creates as well as represses. See, for instance, Michel Foucault, *Discipline and Punish: The Birth of the Prison*, trans. Alan Sheridan (New York: Vintage Books, 1979), 27–8.
81. In *The Birth of the Clinic* Foucault demonstrated that physicians hold power—based upon their professional standing and the authority that accompanies it—to examine patients. Not only does their examination produce knowledge about the individual patient—whether or not the patient is ill, what type of illness the patient suffers from,

and what the treatment should be—but the examination also leads to knowledge, or information, about the population, which can then be used to manage, control, and reconfigure that population. For instance, the examination of a patient suffering from tuberculosis not only gives rise to information about how that patient ought to be treated, but also more broadly-applicable information about how patients contract tuberculosis, how the disease is spread, the relationship between poverty, malnutrition and tuberculosis, the rates of incidence among the middle class versus the working class, and thus the relationship between tuberculosis and working-class life. This information can then be translated into power: new areas of regulation (regulation of factories, work conditions, housing), new policies (both protective and repressive), new forms of policing and social protection. Simultaneously, however, this socially-applicable knowledge produces power for the medical profession as a whole, as well as for the individual practitioner, which reinforces their power and authority to examine patients and collect information/knowledge. Michel Foucault, *The Birth of the Clinic: An Archaeology of Medical Perception*, trans. A. M. Sheridan Smith (New York: Vintage Books, 1975).

82. Dreyfus and Rabinow, *Michael Foucault*, 140.
83. Lynch, *Family, Class, and Ideology in Early Industrial France*, 50. She writes: "Like the Physiocrats, moral economists conceived of economic problems in a way that bound them intimately to the larger question of social governance." She is, I would argue, reiterating Foucault's point that the development of the human sciences concerned with the health of populations (whether political economy, psychiatry, psychology, social work, medicine, penology, etc.) was closely bound up with the problem of how to best govern this population.
84. Ransom, *Foucault's Discipline*, 70.
85. Michel Foucault, *The History of Sexuality, vol. 1: An Introduction*, trans. Robert Hurley (New York: Vintage Books, 1980), 94–5.
86. See Dreyfus and Rabinow, *Michel Foucault*, 187.
87. Again, I am borrowing this definition of government as "a form of activity aimed at shaping other people's conduct" from sociologist Giovanna Procacci in "Governing Poverty: Sources of the Social Question in Nineteenth-Century France," 211.

Chapter Three

1. Andrew Abbott, *The System of Professions: An Essay on the Division of Expert Labor* (Chicago: University of Chicago Press, 1988), 39.
2. John S. Ransom, *Foucault's Discipline: The Politics of Subjectivity* (Durham: Duke University Press, 1997), 25.
3. Honoré Frégier, *Solution nouvelle du problème de la misère, ou moyens pratiques d'améliorer la condition des ouvriers des manufactures et en général des classes laborieuses* (Paris: Amyot, 1851), 9–10.
4. Hippolyte Passy, "Rapport fait à l'Académie des sciences morales et politiques sur le *Manuel d'économie politique* de M. Henri Baudrillart," *Journal des économistes*

[henceforth *JE*], 2d ser., 17 (1858): 47. For another recognition that political economy might be more than just a simple science of wealth, see the statement by Théodore Fix, cited above in the Introduction, from an 1845 issue of the *Journal des économistes.*

5. Henri Baudrillart, "De la méthode en économie politique," *JE,* 3d ser., 1 (1866): 11-31.
6. Horace Say, "Introduction à la deuxième série," *JE,* 2d ser., 1 (1854): 16-17.
7. Terry Nichols Clark, "Émile Durkheim and the Institutionalization of Sociology in the French University System," *Archives Européennes de Sociologie* 9 (1968): 48-49; and Terry Nichols Clark, *Prophets and Patrons: The French University and the Emergence of the Social Sciences* (Cambridge: Harvard University Press, 1973), ch. 6.
8. Clark, "Émile Durkheim," 48-49. The complete quote is as follows: "Indeed, it was characteristic of nineteenth-century social theorists to portray nothing less than the entire universe on their canvases: not content to study such prosaic issues as group cohesion or population movements, they sought to paint all-encompassing frescoes of the history of humanity, explaining its fundamental laws for past and present, and frequently for an idealized future as well."
9. Political economy and sociology were not the only two disciplines that passed through a utopian stage. Jan Goldstein has described the monomania diagnosis as a similar moment in the disciplinary history of French psychiatry. The "aggressively hyperbolic claims" made by mid-nineteenth-century psychiatry attest to the self-confidence of the new science. Jan Goldstein, *Console and Classify: The French Psychiatric Profession in the Nineteenth Century* (Cambridge: Cambridge University Press: 1987), 196.
10. Clark, "Émile Durkheim," 39.
11. Abbott, *The System of Professions,* 71.
12. Ibid., 2.
13. Ibid., 50.
14. Ibid., 63-4.
15. Clark, *Prophets and Patrons,* ch. 1.
16. Abbott, *The System of Professions,* 82. According to Abbott, few professions emerge victorious from a battle over jurisdictional claims without strongly organized professional organizations that can mobilize their members, and act as an effective lobbying structure.
17. Circulation figures for the *Journal des economists* exist for the years 1866-1880. Between those dates, circulation remained steady at 1,400 copies per issue. See Claude Bellanger, et al., *Histoire générale de la presse française,* v. 3 (Paris: Presses Universitaires de France, 1969), 172. Membership figures for the *Société d'économie politique* come from Lucette Le Van-Lemesle, *Le Juste ou le Riche: L'enseignement de l'économie politique, 1815-1950* (Paris: Comité pour l'histoire économique et financière de la France, 2004), 142.
18. Lucette Le Van-Lemesle, "La promotion de l'économie politique en France au dix-neuvième siècle jusqu'à son introduction dans les facultés, 1815-1881." *Revue d'histoire moderne et contemporaine* 27 (April-June 1980): 286.

19. "Protestation de la Société d'économie politique contre la suppression de l'enseignement de l'économie politique," *JE* 20 (1848): 116.
20. One thinks, for instance, of the laws regulating child labor and providing primary education for working-class children. See Katherine Lynch, *Family, Class, and Ideology in Early Industrial France: Social Policy and the Working-Class Family, 1825–1848* (Madison: University of Wisconsin Press, 1988), 168–223.
21. Cited in Edgar Allix, "La méthode et la conception de l'économie politique dans l'oeuvre de Jean-Baptiste Say," *Revue d'histoire des doctrines économiques et sociales* 4 (1911): 353–54.
22. Louis Reybaud, "La condition morale, intellectuelle et matérielle des ouvriers qui vivent de l'industrie du coton," *JE*, 2d ser., 41, no. 26 (April 1862): 63.
23. Ibid., 62.
24. Ibid., 60–1.
25. Louis Reybaud, "La condition morale, intellectuelle et matérielle des ouvriers qui vivent de l'industrie du coton," *JE*, 2d ser., 39, no. 4 (April 1861): 13.
26. Louis Reybaud, "La condition morale, intellectuelle et matérielle des ouvriers qui vivent de l'industrie du coton," *JE*, 2d ser., 40, no. 20 (October 1861): 26.
27. Reybaud, "La condition morale," *JE* (April 1862): 65–6.
28. Louis Reybaud, *Rapport sur la condition morale, intellectuelle et matérielle des ouvriers qui vivent de l'industrie de la laine* (Paris: Didot Frères, 1865), 90.
29. Louis Reybaud, "La condition morale, intellectuelle et matérielle des ouvriers qui vivent de l'industrie du coton," *JE*, 2d ser., 39, no. 2 (February 1861): 79.
30. Reybaud, "La condition morale," *JE* (April 1861): 15.
31. Reybaud, *Rapport*, 91.
32. Ibid., 17.
33. Reybaud, "La condition morale," *JE* (February 1861): 179.
34. Reybaud, "La condition morale," *JE* (April 1862): 70–1.
35. Le Van-Lemesle, "La promotion de l'économie politique en France," 276.
36. Jean-Baptiste-Firmin Marbeau, *Du paupérisme en France et des moyens d'y remédier, ou principes d'économie charitable* (Paris: Comptoir des Imprimeurs-Unis, 1847), 4–9. Similarly, in an 1890 pamphlet, heterodox economist Charles Gide described social economy as the general science of the economic organization of society, and classical political economy, or the "liberal" school, as merely one current in a more general economic science. Charles Gide, *Quatres écoles d'économie sociale* (Genève: Stapelmohr, 1890).
37. *Annales de la Société d'économie politique* 7 (May 1867): 152–53. Garnier's reference back to Greek and Latin was reiterated several years later by Ambroise Clément in the pages of the *Journal des économistes*, with the similar conclusion that political economy and social economy were synonyms. Ambroise Clément, "Observations sur la nomenclature économique," *JE*, 3rd ser., 62 (1872): 9.
38. More than a decade earlier, in 1855, at another meeting of the *Société d'économie politique*, Garnier, in fact, *bemoaned* the plethora of synonyms often used for political economy—including *économie sociale*—arguing that he preferred the term *l'économique* to any other. The point here, of course, is that even individual political

economists seldom remained consistent in the way that they defined their terms. *Annales de la Société d'économie politique* 2 (April 1855): 160.

39. "Louis Bianchini, *Principes de la science du bien-être sociale, de l'économie publique et de l'économie des états*: compte rendu par A. Leymarie," *JE*, 2d ser., 21 (1859): 226–32.

40. *Annales de la Société d'économie politique* 7 (May 1867): 144–59.

41. Ibid., 146.

42. Ibid., 147.

43. Ibid., 152–53.

44. For some historical work on social economy, see Leora Auslander, *Taste and Power: Furnishing Modern France* (Berkeley: University of California Press, 1996); Katherine Lynch, *Family, Class, and Ideology in Early Industrial France: Social Policy and the Working-Class Family, 1825–1848* (Madison: University of Wisconsin Press, 1988); Janet R. Horne, *A Social Laboratory for Modern France: The Musée Social and the Rise of the Welfare State* (Durham: Duke University Press, 2002); Jacques Donzelot, *The Policing of Families* (New York: Random House, 1979); François Ewald, *L'État providence* (Paris: Éditions Grasset, 1986); and Giovanna Procacci, *Gouverner la Misère: La question sociale en France, 1789–1848* (Paris: Éditions du Seuil, 1993).

45. Procacci, *Gouverner la Misère*, 164.

46. Adolphe Blaise, "Cours d'économie politique du Collège de France par M. Michel Chevalier," *JE* 1 (1841): 205.

47. Ibid., 206.

48. Debates about whether a particular subject ought to be studied as a science or an art were not limited to political economy. In fact, an interesting parallel seems to exist between political economy's struggle to determine its status and a similar struggle in medicine. Claude Bernard's *Introduction à l'étude de la medicine expérimentale*, and Émile Zola's commentary on Bernard's text, *Le roman experimental*, both suggest that nineteenth-century doctors as well as certain writers were ruminating upon whether medicine and literature had moved beyond the domain of pure art and had finally entered the arena of science. I am grateful to Jan Goldstein, Alex Dracobly, and Claudine Frank for drawing my attention to the art and science dichotomy in nineteenth-century medical discourse. If Claude Bernard championed the triumph of scientific methods within the medical profession, however, many Third Republic physicians were actually much less comfortable with cold-hearted science and sought instead to emphasize the hands-on element of their profession, the personal, idiosyncratic, and artistic elements. Martha Hildreth, "The Balzac Revival in the Early Third Republic: Reconstructing the Doctor's Role in the Culture Wars over Science" (paper presented at the annual international meeting of the Western Society for French History, Lubbock, Texas, November 2004).

49. Charles Coquelin, "Économie politique," *Dictionnaire de l'économie politique*, Charles Coquelin and G.-U. Guillaumin, eds. (Paris: Guillaumin, 1852–3), 1:645.

50. See Fernand Faure, "Science and Art," *Nouveau dictionnaire d'économie politique*, Léon Say and Joseph Chailley, eds. (Paris: Guillaumin, 1891–2), 2:796–97; Joseph

Chailley-Bert, "Introduction," *Nouveau dictionnaire*, 1:v; and Courcelle-Seneuil, "Économie politique," *Nouveau dictionnaire*, 1:764–65.

51. Clément, "Introduction," *Dictionnaire*, 1:*xiv*.
52. Courcelle-Seneuil, "Science, application, enseignement de l'économie politique," *JE*, 4th ser., 73, no. 5 (May 1878): 225–43.
53. Coquelin, "Économie politique," *Dictionnaire*, 1:646.
54. Courcelle-Seneuil, "Économie politique," *Nouveau dictionnaire*, 1:764.
55. Coquelin, "Économie politique," *Dictionnaire*, 1:647.
56. Courcelle-Seneuil, "Économie politique," *Nouveau dictionnaire*, 1:770.
57. Hippolyte Passy, "*De l'économie publique et de ses rapports avec la morale et le droit*, par M. Minghetti," *JE*, ser. 2, 40 (1861): 196–97.
58. Ibid., 202.
59. *Annales de la Société d'économie politique* 5 (January 5, 1864): 452–53.
60. See, for instance, the minutes of the September 6, 1886 meeting of the Société d'économie politique, devoted to the question of whether political economy was a science distinct from morality and law. *Annales de la Société d'économie politique* 15 (1886).
61. *Annales de la Société d'économie politique* 2 (December 9, 1854): 104.
62. Henri Baudrillart, while saving his most direct criticisms for Jean-Baptiste Say, faulted even Adam Smith for having too quickly abandoned the human character of political economy: "Why would Adam Smith himself, who, while opening his *The Wealth of Nations* with the picture of the division of labor, so magnificently demonstrated that he understood the predominance of man in production, not engage completely with this fecund inspiration instead of throwing himself, almost from the beginning, into digressions which removed from his book the authority of method, and in which the human character of political economy disappeared a bit too soon from the research of material facts." Baudrillart, "De la méthode en économie politique," 19–20.
63. Of course, more recent assessments of Jean-Baptiste Say's economic thought would challenge Courcelle-Seneuil's judgments.
64. Courcelle-Seneuil, "Aperçu historique sur l'économie politique," *Nouveau dictionnaire*, 1:782.
65. For Foucault, the primary difference between the physical sciences and the human sciences resides in the physical sciences' supposed success in divorcing themselves from the political and historical circumstances—in Foucault's words, the "background practices"—out of which they emerged. Whereas, according to Foucault, the natural sciences have been able to move beyond these background practices, separating themselves from the intersection between power/knowledge, divorcing power from knowledge, and thus residing in the realm of knowledge alone, the human sciences are hopelessly and perhaps intrinsically, bound up in the power/knowledge nexus. See Hubert L. Dreyfus and Paul Rabinow, *Michel Foucault: Beyond Structuralism and Hermeneutics* (Chicago: The University of Chicago Press, 1982), 160–64. The terms "muddled" and "successful" sciences are Dreyfus and Rabinow's. Dreyfus and Rabinow, *Michel Foucault*, 177.

Chapter Four

1. Lucette Le Van-Lemesle, *Le Juste ou le Riche: L'enseignement de l'économie politique, 1815–1950* (Paris: Comité pour l'histoire économique et financière de la France, 2004), 257.
2. According to Foucault, "perhaps one should reverse the problem and ask oneself what is served by the failure of the prison; what is the use of these different phenomena that are continually being criticized; the maintenance of delinquency, the encouragement of recidivism, the transformation of the occasional offender into a habitual delinquent...one would be forced to suppose that the prison, and no doubt punishment in general, is not intended to eliminate offences, but rather to distinguish them, to distribute them, to use them." Michel Foucault, *Discipline and Punish: The Birth of the Prison,* trans. Alan Sheridan (New York: Vintage Books, 1979), 272.
3. The letter was originally published as Jean-Baptiste Say, "Lettre inédite sur l'utilité d'établir l'enseignement de l'économie politique dans les écoles industrielles," *Journal des économistes* [henceforth *JE*] 13, no. 53 (April 1846).
4. For the history of the chair in political economy established in 1864 at the *Faculté de Droit de Paris,* and for its regularization in 1877, I am relying upon Lucette Le Van-Lemesle. See Le Van-Lemesle, *Le Juste ou le Riche,* 259–321.
5. Ibid., 173–4.
6. Ibid., 173.
7. Ibid., 173–74.
8. Ibid., 284.
9. Ibid., ch. 11.
10. Charles Gide, "The Economic Schools and the Teaching of Political Economy in France," *Political Science Quarterly* 5, no. 4 (1890): 603–35.
11. For a more complete discussion of Cauwès and his course at the *Faculté de Droit de Paris,* see chapters 8 and 9 in Le Van-Lemesle, *Le Juste ou le Riche.*
12. Le Van-Lemesle, *Le Juste ou le Riche,* 276.
13. Ibid.
14. Gide, "The Economic Schools," 603–35.
15. See Le Van-Lemesle, *Le Juste ou le Riche,* 311-16, for her discussion of the *Revue d'économie politique* and its contributors. For another discussion of the *Revue d'économie politique,* see Luc Marco and Evelyne Laurent, *Le Journal des économistes, 1841–1940* (Paris: Éditions de l'Association Nationale des Docteur ès Sciences Economiques, 1990).
16. Charles Gide, "Chronique," *Revue d'économie politique* 1 (1887): 73.
17. Ibid., 89.
18. Ibid., 83.
19. Le Van-Lemesle, *Le Juste ou le Riche,* 309.
20. Courcelle-Seneuil, "Situation et perspectives de l'économie politique," *JE* (Sept. 1877): 313–29. Originally cited in Le Van-Lemesle, *Le Juste ou le Riche,* 299–300.
21. Gide, "Chronique," 84.

22. The end of the nineteenth century saw the explosion of the social, or the human, sciences. Sociology is, of course, the best known, but other social scientific disciplines were gaining professional status by the end of the century: statistics, criminology, psychology, anthropology, social work. Linking these diverse human sciences was the effort to find "the modern cure for the pathologies of modernity," to borrow the words of historian Ann-Louise Shapiro. Ann-Louise Shapiro, *Breaking the Codes: Female Criminality in Fin-de-Siècle Paris* (Stanford: Stanford University Press, 1996): 17.
23. This exchange was first cited in Lucette Le Van-Lemesle's *Le Juste ou le Riche*, 288–97. She uses the exchange as evidence of the opposition encountered by economists from some jurists. I am using the exchange to illuminate a rather different phenomenon.
24. Courcelle-Seneuil, "Économie politique," *Nouveau dictionnaire d'économie politique*, Léon Say and Joseph Chailley, eds. (Paris: Guillaumin, 1891–2), 1:770.
25. It is almost as if in 1877, Courcelle-Seneuil was defending political economy as the type of science that Italian economist Louis Bianchini, whose book had been reviewed in the *Journal des économistes* in 1859, would have embraced. Bianchini referred to political economy as a "social science," and even more precisely as a "science of social well-being." This social science was composed of an amalgam of economic principles, legal and ethical principles, political and administrative practices. As Bianchini described it, political economy was not only compatible with the law, but it was an indispensable partner, devoted as it was to social well-being. "Louis Bianchini, *Principes de la science du bien-être sociale, de l'économie publique et de l'économie des états*: compte rendu par A. Leymarie," *JE*, 2d ser., 21 (1859): 226–32. See my chapter 3 for for a discussion of Bianchini and the *Journal des économistes* review.
26. Charles Gide, "Les doctrines économiques de M. Charles Périn," *JE*, 4th ser., 82 (1882): 30–40.
27. Henri Baudrillart, "L'économie sociale et l'économie politique," *JE*, 4th ser., 91 (1887): 329–44.
28. Christian Topalov, "Les 'réformateurs' et leurs réseaux: enjeux d'un objet de recherché," in Christian Topalov, ed., *Laboratoires du nouveau siècle: La nébuleuse réformatrice et ses réseaux en France, 1880–1914* (Paris: Éditions de l'École des hautes études en sciences sociales, 1999), 37.
29. Le Van-Lemesle, *Le Juste ou le Riche*, 420.
30. Ibid., 423-4.
31. Topalov, "Les 'réformateurs' et leurs réseaux," 37. Topalov himself is citing from H. Hauser, *L'enseignement des sciences sociales: État actuel de cet enseignement dans les divers pays du monde* (Paris: A. Chevalier-Maresq, 1903), 165.
32. Le Van-Lemesle, *Le Juste ou le Riche*, 399. Le Van-Lemesle notes that even while Cheysson taught *économie politique*, he taught students about topics that fell under the rubric of *économie sociale*. Cheysson introduced his students to topics such as labor, low-income housing, workers' gardens, and *crèches* (nursery schools), and even took students to visit factories and working-class homes. Cheysson had once worked

as a director for the *Établissements Schneider* in Le Creusot, one of France's premier paternalist factory towns, and thus it is not surprising to find his instruction in political economy profoundly influenced by social economic concerns.

33. George Weisz, "L'idéologie républicaine et les sciences sociales: Les durkheimiens et la chaire d'histoire d'économie sociale à la Sorbonne," *Revue française de sociologie* 20 (1979): 83–112.
34. Giovanna Procacci, *Gouverner la Misère: La question sociale en France, 1789–1848* (Paris: Éditions du Seuil, 1993), 164.
35. Janet R. Horne, *A Social Laboratory for Modern France: The Musée Social and the Rise of the Welfare State* (Durham: Duke University Press, 2002), 5.
36. Ibid., 43.
37. A. Le Roux, *Nouvel ordre de récompenses institué en faveur des établissements et des localités qui ont développé la bonne harmonie entre les personnes coopérant aux mêmes travaux, et qui ont assuré aux ouvriers le bien-être matériel, intellectuel et moral* (Paris: Imprimerie administratif de Paul Dupont, 1867), 9–10.
38. Ibid., 14.
39. Topalov, "Les 'réformateurs' et leurs réseaux," 13.
40. Ibid., 37–9.
41. The literature on governmentality is now abundant. See, among others, Mitchell Dean, *Governmentality: Power and Rule in Modern Society* (London: SAGE Publications, 1999); John S. Ransom, *Foucault's Discipline: The Politics of Subjectivity* (Durham: Duke University Press, 1997); Graham Burchell, Colin Gordon, and Peter Miller, eds., *The Foucault Effect: Studies in Governmentality* (Chicago: The University of Chicago Press, 1991); Michel Foucault, *Power: The Essential Works of Foucault, 1954–1984* (New York: The New Press, 2000); and Michel Foucault, *Security, Territory, Population: Lectures at the Collège de France, 1977-1978* (London: Palgrave MacMillan, 2007).
42. Dean, *Governmentality*, 2.
43. Ibid., 10–11.
44. Ibid., 12.
45. Ibid., 20.
46. Dean refers to these forms of knowledge cooperating with (that is, arising from and informing) the practices of government as the "episteme of government." Ibid., 31.
47. The source of my questions is Mitchell Dean's proposal that an analysis of government should be "concerned with the means of calculation, both qualitative and quantitative, the type of governing authority or agency, the forms of knowledge, techniques and other means employed, the entity to be governed and how it is conceived, the ends sought and the outcomes and consequences." Ibid., 11.
48. Adam Smith, *An Inquiry into the Nature and Causes of the Wealth of Nations* (New York: The Modern Library, 1937), 66–7.
49. Dean, *Governmentality*, 12.
50. Interest in this topic is usually understood as having been provoked by the three volumes of *The History of Sexuality* by Michel Foucault. See Michel Foucault, *The History of Sexuality: An Introduction* (New York: Pantheon Books, 1978); *The Use*

of Pleasure (New York: Pantheon Books, 1985); and *The Care of the Self* (New York: Pantheon Books, 1986).

51. Hubert L. Dreyfus and Paul Rabinow, *Michel Foucault: Beyond Structuralism and Hermeneutics* (Chicago: The University of Chicago Press, 1982), 187.

Conclusion

1. Louis Reybaud, "Introduction," *Journal des économistes* [henceforth *JE*] 1 (1841): 9.
2. Joyce Appleby, Lynn Hunt, and Margaret Jacob, *Telling the Truth About History* (New York: W.W. Norton, 1994), 15.
3. Lucette Le Van-Lemesle, *Le Juste ou le Riche: L'enseignement de l'économie politique, 1815–1950* (Paris: Comité pour l'histoire économique et financière de la France, 2004), 633.
4. Théodore Fix, "De la manière d'observer les faits économiques," *JE* 12 (1845): 98.
5. Charles Gide, "Chronique," *Revue d'économie politique* 1 (1887): 84.

Selected Bibliography

Archival Sources

France. Académie François Bourdon. Le Creusot.

01L0075 Rapports sur la grève de 1899 et 1900
FX/0017 Grèves
SS/0299 Oeuvres sociales, 1929–1930
SS/0232 Oeuvres sociales
DH/0009-14 Dossiers historiques
SS/420 Logements ouvriers
01L018 Régistre statistique

France. Archives de la Société Mulhousienne des cités ouvrières. Centre Rhénan d'Archives et de Recherches Économiques. Mulhouse.

A/1420 Rapports sur les logements, 1853–1922
A/1425 Prix Salathé pour encouragement de la classe ouvrière à l'économie, 1911–1914

France. Archives départementales du Haut-Rhin. Colmar.

1/M/66 Rapports périodiques du sous-préfet d'Altkirch, 1800–1870
1/M/69 Rapports sur la situation des communes, 1829–1863
4/M/46 Agitation dans les communes, 1843–1870
8/M/32 Exposition universelle de 1867 à Paris
9/M/24 Cités ouvrières de Mulhouse, 1853–1868
10/M/1-3 Règlements internes des manufactures
10/M/4-5 Travail des enfants dans les manufactures
10/M/6 Enquête de 1848–49 sur le travail
10/M/7 Crises industrielles
10/M/8-9 Conflits du travail
10/M/10 Rapports d'accidents
10/M/11 Moralité et instruction des classes ouvrières
1/T/87-89 Enseignement primaire
1/T/548-9 Bibliothèque et cours populaires de Guebwiller et Mulhouse
1/T/1451 Enseignement primaire à Mulhousc

4/X/30 Caisses d'épargne
1/Z/513 Conflits du travail, 1804–70
1/Z/1535 Société d'encouragement à l'épargne de Mulhouse et caisses d'épargne

France. Archives départementales du Saône-et-Loire. Mâcon.

M/8-11 Rapports des Sous-Préfets, 1857–1862
M/9 Rapports des Préfets, 1870–1878
M/20 Rapports des Sous-Préfets, 1894–1909
M/109 Émeutes, troubles saint-simoniens, 1830–1848
M/118 Situation politique de l'arrondissement
M/146 Commissaires spéciaux d'Autun et du Creusot
M/147 Commissaire spéciale de Montceau-les-Mines
M/152-4 Police générale
M/158 Funerailles de M. Eugène Schneider
M/169 Police générale, Montceau-les-Mines, 1902
M/3285-7 Grèves au Creusot
M/3296 Grèves au Montceau-les-Mines

France. Archives des houillères de Blanzy. Montceau-les-Mines.

Carton 1 Miscellaneous information

France. Archives municipales de Mulhouse. Mulhouse.

J/II/Hf1 Coalitions, 1827–1831
J/II/Hr4 Émeutes et grèves, 1847–1848
Q/III/K1 Cités ouvrières
Q/IV/Aa3 Caisse d'épargne
Q/V/Bc Mutuelles de secours de plusieurs industriels
Q/V/Cd5 État des caisses de secours
R/I/Cb2 Écoles pour les ouvriers

France. Archives nationales.

AJ/16/1791 Académie de Paris
AQ/92/1-31 Société Anonyme des Mines de Houille de Blanzy
AQ/187/1-13 Archives de la Société Schneider et Compagnie
BB/18/1409 Desordres à la fabrique de Breitenbach
BB/18/1479 Le Creusot, grève de 1850
BB/18/1648 Grève à Sainte-Marie-aux-Mines, 1862
BB/24/721 Luttes sanglantes entre ouvriers français et ouvriers piémontais
BB/24/722 Dégradation d'une fontaine sur la place de l'église à Guebwiller, 1869
BB/24/724 Émeute et manifestation contre l'Hôtel de Ville, Mulhouse, 1870

BB/30/376–77 Rapports du Procureur Général de Colmar
BB/30/389–90 Rapports des Procureurs Générales
BB/30/420 Agitation ouvrière au Creusot, 1858
F1/c/III/Haut-Rhin/7 Comptes-rendus administratifs
F1/c/III/Haut-Rhin/13–14 Correspondance et divers
F/7/12526 Troubles à Montceau-les-Mines
F/7/12765 Industrie métallurgique: questions ouvrières
F/7/12782 Mineurs, Département du Saône-et-Loire
F/7/12848 Catastrophe de Montceau-les-Mines, 1895
F/12/3767–3768 Exposition Universelle de 1889: Économie Sociale
F/12/4356 Exposition Universelle de 1900: Palais des Femmes
F/12/4704–4706 Loi de 22 Mars 1841
F/17/13556 Collège de France

France. Écomusée du Creusot. Le Creusot.

A/41 Écoles du Creusot
A/44 Règlements de l'usine
A/249 Écoles ménagères
A/271 Projet des jardins ouvriers
A/291 Schneider et Compagnie, Règlement générale, 1913
A/348 Cahiers écoliers
A/357 Cahier scolaire, École Ménagère, 1912
A/481 École de Filles des Mines de Blanzy, 1913–1917
A/754 Directions pédagogiques aux maîtres des Écoles Schneider, 1909

Printed Primary Sources

Allix, Edgar. "Jean-Baptiste Say et les origines de l'industrialisme." *Revue d'économie politique* 24 (1910): 303–63.

———. "La déformation de l'économie politique libérale après Jean-Baptiste Say: Charles Dunoyer." *Revue d'histoire des doctrines économiques et sociales* 4 (1911): 115–47.

———. "La méthode et la conception de l'économie politique dans l'oeuvre de Jean-Baptiste Say." *Revue d'histoire des doctrines économiques et sociales* 4 (1911): 321–60.

Annales de la Société d'économie politique.

Bastiat, Frédéric. *Harmonies économiques.* Paris: Guillaumin, 1851.

Baudrillart, Henri. *Des rapports de la morale et de l'économie politique. Cours professé au Collège de France.* Paris: Guillaumin, 1860.

———. *L'amélioration des logements d'ouvriers dans ses rapports avec l'esprit de famille.* Paris: A. Picard, 1889.

Blanqui, Jerome Adolphe. *Cours d'économie industrielle, 1836–1837.* Paris: J. Angé, 1837.

———. *Cours d'économie industrielle, 1837–1838.* Paris: J. Angé, 1838.

———. *Cours d'économie industrielle, 1838–1839.* Paris: J. Angé, 1839.

Boyer, Adolphe. *De l'état des ouvriers et de son amélioration par l'organisation du travail.* Paris: Dubois, 1841.

Bulletin de la Société Industrielle de Mulhouse.

Burat, Amedée. *Société des Houillères de Blanzy: situation de ses établissements en 1877.* Paris: J. Baudry, 1878.

———. *Notice sur les institutions ouvrières des mines de Blanzy.* Dijon: Imprimerie de l'Union Typographique, 1893.

Buret, Eugène. *De la misère des classes laborieuses en Angleterre et en France. De la nature de la misère, de son existence, de ses effets, de ses causes, et de l'insuffisance des remèdes qu'on lui a opposés jusqu'ici; avec l'indication des moyens propres à en affranchir les sociétés.* 2 vols. Paris: Paulin, 1840.

Centenaire de la Société Industrielle de Mulhouse, 1826–1926. 2 vols. Mulhouse: Braun et Compagnie, 1926.

Cetty, Abbé Henri. *La famille ouvrière en Alsace.* Rixheim: Imprimerie de A. Sutter, 1883.

———. *Le mariage dans les classes ouvrières.* Rixheim: Imprimerie de A. Sutter, 1885.

Chagot, Jules. *Note sur les houillères de Blanzy et sur les institutions spéciales pour développer le bien-être matériel et moral des ouvriers.* Paris: Imprimerie Guyot et Scribe, 1867.

———. *Notice sur les institutions ouvrières des mines de Blanzy.* Lyon: Imprimerie du Salut Public, 1890.

Cheysson, Émile. *Le Creusot: condition moral, matérielle et intellectuelle de la population.* Paris: P. Dupont, 1869.

———. *La question des habitations ouvrières en France et à l'étranger.* Paris, G. Masson, 1886.

———. *Exposition universelle internationale de 1889 à Paris. Groupe d'économie sociale. Section XVI: Institutions patronales.* Paris: Imprimerie nationale, 1892.

Congrès Régional des oeuvres d'assistance, de prévoyance, et d'assurance sociales. *Congrès des oeuvres sociales.* Lille: n.p., 1910.

Coquelin, Charles, and G.-U. Guillaumin, eds. *Dictionnaire de l'économie politique.* 2 vols. Paris: Guillaumin, 1852–53.

Courcelle-Seneuil, Jean-Gustave. *Traité théorique et pratique des entreprises industrielles, commérciales et agricoles, ou Manuel des affaires.* Paris: Guillaumin, 1855.

Courtois, Félix. *Les écoles du Creusot, 1787–1882.* Autun: Imprimerie Dejussieu, 1893.

Deseilligny, A. P. *De l'influence de l'éducation sur la moralité et le bien-être des classes laborieuses.* Paris: Hachette, 1868.

Dollfus, Émile. *Les dispositions prises par l'industrie en faveur de ses ouvriers et employés.* Paris: Imprimerie de Vaugirard, 1933.

Dollfus, Jean. *Note sur les cités ouvrières.* Paris: Imprimerie de E., n.d.

Dubois, Dr. *Rapports sur le service de santé des mines de Blanzy et du Montceau.* Paris: Imprimerie Bailly, Divry, et Compagnie, 1855.

Dufau, P.-A. "Mémoire sur la conciliation de l'économie politique et de l'économie charitable ou assistance." *Séances et travaux de l'Académie des sciences morales et politique* 51 (1860): 89–117.

Dumay, Jean-Baptiste. *Mémoires d'un militant ouvrier du Creusot, 1841–1905.* Paris: F. Maspero, 1976.

Dunoyer, Charles. *L'industrie et la morale considerées dans leurs rapports avec la liberté.* Paris: A. Sautelet, 1825.

———. *De la liberté du travail ou simple exposé des conditions dans lesquelles les forces humaines s'exercent avec le plus de puissance.* Paris: Guillaumin, 1845.

Économie sociale: institutions de MM. Schneider et Compagnie. Nevers: Imprimerie Mazeron Frères, 1905.

Engel-Dollfus, Frédéric. *Étude sur l'épargne, les institutions de prévoyance et la participation des bénéfices.* Mulhouse: Imprimerie Veuve Bader, 1876.

Enquête décennale sur les institutions d'initiative privée destinées à favoriser l'amélioration de l'état matériel et moral de la population de la Haute-Alsace: Rapport présenté à la Société industrielle par son comité d'utilité publique à l'occasion de l'Exposition Universelle de 1878. Mulhouse: Imprimerie de Veuve Bader, 1878.

Enquête décennale sur les institutions d'utilité publique de la Haute-Alsace: Rapports présentés à la Société industrielle par son comité d'utilité publique. Mulhouse: Imprimerie Veuve Bader, 1889.

Établissements Schneider et Compagnie. *Le Creusot: son industrie, sa population.* Paris: Imprimerie Centrale des Chemins de Fer, 1867.

Exposition universelle de 1867 à Paris. Rapports du jury international. Vol. 13. Groupe 10, Classes 89 à 95. Habitations caraterisées par le bon marché uni aux conditions d'hygiène et de bien-être. Paris: Imprimerie administrative de Paul Dupont, 1868.

Forest, Jean. *L'emprise.* Paris: La pensée universelle, 1971.

Frégier, Honoré. *Solution nouvelle du problème de la misère, ou moyens pratiques d'améliorer la condition des ouvriers des manufactures et en général des classes laborieuses.* Paris: Amyot, 1851.

Garnier, Joseph. *Tableau des causes de la misère et des remèdes qu'on peut y apporter.* Paris: Garnier Frères, 1858.

———. *De l'origine et de la filation du mot 'économie politique' et des divers autres noms donnés à la science économique.* Paris: Guillaumin, 1852.

Gide, Charles. *Principes d'économie politique.* Paris: L. Larose et Forcel, 1884.

———. *Quatres écoles d'économie sociale, conférences données à l'aula de l'Université de Genève sous les auspices de la Société chrétienne suisse d'économie sociale.* Genève: Stapelmohr, 1890.

———. "The Economic Schools and the Teaching of Political Economy in France." *Political Science Quarterly* 5, no. 4 (1890): 603–35.

———. *Si les institutions sociales sont un mal social.* Paris: L. Larose, 1899.

———. *Économie sociale.* Paris: L. Larose et L. Tenin, 1905.

Gide, Charles, and Charles Rist, eds. *A History of Economic Doctrines from the time of the Physiocrats to the Present Day.* 7th edition. Boston: D. C. Heath, 1948.

Grad, Charles. *Études statistiques sur l'industrie de l'Alsace.* 2 vols. Strasbourg: Librairie Noiriel, 1897.

Husson, François. *La seconde révolution française: solution et dénouement pacifique de la question sociale ouvrière.* Paris: Guillaumin, 1892.

Journal des économistes.

Le Grand, Daniel. *Lettre d'un industriel des montagnes des Vosges.* Paris: F.G. Levrault, 1838.

———. *Appel respectueux d'un industriel de la vallée des Vosges adressé aux gouvernements de la France, de l'Angleterre, de la Prusse, des autres états de l'Allemagne, et de la Suisse: dans le but de provoquer des lois particuliers et une loi internationale, destinées à proteger la classe ouvrière contre le travail précoce et excessif, cause première et principale de son dépérissement physique, de son abrutissement moral, et de sa privation des benedictions de la vie de famille.* Strasbourg: Imprimerie de Berger-Levrault, 1848.

———. *Appel respectueux adressé aux gouvernements des pays industriels dans le but de provoquer une loi internationale sur le travail industriel.* Strasbourg: C. Fasoli et Ohlman, 1855.

LePlay, Frédéric. *La réforme sociale en France déduite de l'observation comparée des peuples européens.* 2 vols. Tours: Alfred Mame et Fils, 1864.

LeRoux, A. *Nouvel ordre de récompenses institué en faveur des établissements et des localités qui ont développé la bonne harmonie entre les personnes coopérant aux mêmes travaux, et qui ont assuré aux ouvriers le bien-être matériel, intellectuel et moral.* Paris: Imprimerie administratif de Paul Dupont, 1867.

Les Établissements Schneider: Économie sociale. Paris: Imprimerie Générale Lahure, 1912.

Levasseur, Émile. *L'enseignement de l'économie politique au Conservatoire des arts et métiers.* Paris: A. Chevalier-Marescq et Compagnie, 1901.

Marbeau, Jean-Baptiste-Firmin. *Du paupérisme en France et des moyens d'y remédier, ou principes d'économie charitable.* Paris: Comptoir des Imprimeurs-Unis, 1847.

Mines de Blanzy. *Règlement sur les logements d'employés et d'ouvriers.* Le Creusot: Imprimerie de A. Temporal, 1871.

Muller, Émile and Émile Cacheux. *Les habitations ouvrières en tous pays, situation en 1871, avenir.* Paris: J. Dejey et Compagnie, 1879.

Nouvelle Biographie Génerale. Paris: Firmin-Didot Frères, 1857.

Pecqueur, Constantin. *Économie sociale. Des intérêts du commerce, de l'industrie et de l'agriculture, et de la civilisation en général, sous l'influence des applications de la vapeur.* 2 vols. Paris: Desessart, 1839.

Penot, Achille. *Les cités ouvrières de Mulhouse et du département du Haut-Rhin.* Mulhouse: Imprimerie de L.L. Bader, 1867.

Picot, Georges. *Les institutions patronales en France et la lutte contre le socialisme.* Paris: Sécretariat de la Société d'économie sociale, 1890.

Rapport de la Commission d'examen des produits industriels de Saône-et-Loire, sur l'Établissement du Creuzot. Mâcon: Imprimerie de Dejuissieu, 1849.

Revue d'économie politique.

Reybaud, Louis. *Études sur le régime des manufactures: condition des ouvriers en soie.* Paris: Michel Lévy Frères, 1859.

———. "Les chaires d'économie politique en France." *Revue des deux mondes* 54 (1864): 948–78.

———. *Rapport sur la condition morale, intellectuelle et matérielle des ouvriers qui vivent de l'industrie de la laine.* Paris: Didot Frères, 1865.

———. *Rapport sur la condition morale, intellectuelle et matérielle des ouvriers qui vivent de l'industrie du fer.* Paris: Didot Frères, 1872.

Say, Jean-Baptiste. *Traité d'économie politique, ou simple exposition de la manière dont se forment, se distribuent, et se consomment les richesses.* Paris: Deterville, 1803.

Say, Léon. *Exposition universelle de 1889 à Paris. Rapports du Jury Internationale. Groupe de l'Économie sociale. Rapport général.* Paris: Imprimerie nationale, 1891.

Say, Léon and Joseph Chailley, eds. *Nouveau dictionnaire d'économie politique.* 2 vols. Paris: Guillaumin, 1891.

Simonin, Louis. *La grande industrie française: l'usine du Creusot.* Paris: E. Lacroix, 1866.

Smith, Adam. *An Inquiry into the Nature and Causes of the Wealth of Nations.* New York: The Modern Library, 1937.

Société Anonyme des Mines de Houille de Blanzy. *Hôpital des blessés, consultation des nourrissons et goutte de lait: oeuvre du trousseau dans les écoles de filles.* Montceau: Rajaud Frères, 1910.

Thierry-Mieg, Charles. *Réflections sur l'amélioration morale des classes ouvrières.* Mulhouse: Imprimerie de P. Barat, 1860.

———. *Rapport sur les forces matérielles et morales de l'industrie du Haut-Rhin pendant les dix dernières années.* Mulhouse: Imprimerie de P. Barat, 1862.

Veron, Eugène. *Les institutions ouvrières de Mulhouse et des environs.* Paris: Hachette, 1866.

Villermé, Louis-René. *Tableau de l'état physique et moral des ouvriers employés dans les manufactures de coton, de laine et de soie.* 2 vols. Paris: Jules Renouard, 1840.

———. "Sur les cités ouvrières." *Annales de l'hygiène publique et de médicine légale* 43 (1850): 241-61.

Secondary Sources

Abbott, Andrew. *The System of Professions: An Essay on the Division of Expert Labor.* Chicago: The University of Chicago Press, 1988.

Alcorn, Stanley, and Ben Solarz. "The Autistic Economist." *Yale Economic Review: A Yale University Student Publication* (Summer 2006), http://www.yaleeconomicreview.com/issues/2006_summer/autistic_economist.html.

Appleby, Joyce, Lynn Hunt, and Margaret Jacob. *Telling the Truth About History.* New York: W.W. Norton, 1994.

Auslander, Leora. *Taste and Power: Furnishing Modern France.* Berkeley: University of California Press, 1996.

Backhouse, Roger E. *The Ordinary Business of Life: A History of Economics from the Ancient World to the Twenty-First Century.* Princeton: Princeton University Press, 2002.

Bellanger, Claude, Jacques Godechot, Pierre Guiral, and Fernand Terrou. *Histoire générale de la presse française.* 5 vols. Paris: Presses Universitaires de France, 1969.

Bergeron, Louis. *Les capitalistes en France, 1780-1914.* Paris: Gallimard, 1978.

Borghese, Arthur. "Industrialist Paternalism and Lower-Class Agitation: The Case of Mulhouse, 1848–1851." *Histoire Sociale/Social History* 25 (1980): 55–84.

Breton, Yves. "Les économistes, le pouvoir politique et l'ordre social en France entre 1830 et 1851." *Histoire, Économie, et Société* 2 (1985): 233–52.

Breton, Yves, and Michel Lutfalla, eds. *L'économie politique en France au dix-neuvième siècle.* Paris: Economica, 1992.

Bullock, Nicholas, and James Read. *The Movement for Housing Reform in Germany and France, 1840–1914.* Cambridge: Cambridge University Press, 1985.

Burchell, Graham, Colin Gordon, and Peter Miller, eds. *The Foucault Effect: Studies in Governmentality.* Chicago: The University of Chicago Press, 1991.

Burdeau, Georges. *Le libéralisme.* Paris: Éditions Seuil, 1979.

Campbell, Deborah. "Kick it Over! The Rise of Post-Autistic Economics." *Adbusters* 5 (2004), http://adbusters.org/the_magazine/55/Kick_it_Over_The_Rise_of_PostAutistic Economics.html.

Chevalier, Louis. *Classes laborieuses et classes dangereuses à Paris pendant la première moitié du dix-neuvième siècle.* Paris: Hachette, 1978.

Clark, Terry Nichols. "Émile Durkheim and the Institutionalization of Sociology in the French University System." *Archives Européennes de Sociologie* 9 (1968): 37–71.

———. *Prophets and Patrons: The French University and the Emergence of the Social Sciences.* Cambridge: Harvard University Press, 1973.

Coleman, William. *Death is a Social Disease: Public Health and Political Economy in Early Industrial France.* Madison: University of Wisconsin Press, 1982.

Cottereau, Alain. "Les règlements d'atelier au cours de la révolution industrielle en France." Anne Biroleau, ed. *Les règlements d'ateliers, 1798–1936.* Paris: Bibliothèque Nationale, 1984.

Dean, Mitchell. *Governmentality: Power and Rule in Modern Society.* London: Sage Publications, 1999.

Démier, Francis. "Adolphe Blanqui, un économiste fâce à la révolution industrielle, 1794–1854." Thèse de troisième cycle, Université de Paris X, 1979.

Devillers, Christian, and Bernard Huet. *Le Creusot: naissance et développement d'une ville industrielle, 1782-1914.* Seyssel: Champ Vallon, 1981.

Dewerpe, Alain. *Le monde du travail en France, 1800-1950.* Paris: Armand Colin, 1989.

Donzelot, Jacques. *The Policing of Families.* Robert Hurley, trans. New York: Random House, 1979.

Dreyfus, Hubert L., and Paul Rabinow. *Michel Foucault: Beyond Structuralism and Hermeneutics.* Chicago: The University of Chicago Press, 1982.

Duroselle, Jean-Baptiste. *Les débuts du catholicisme sociale en France, 1822-1870.* Paris: Presses universitaires de France, 1951.

Elwitt, Sanford. *The Third Republic Defended: Bourgeois Reform in France, 1880-1914.* Baton Rouge: Louisiana State University Press, 1986.

Ewald, François. *L'État providence.* Paris: Éditions Grasset, 1986.

Fontanon, Claudine, and André Grelon, eds. *Les Professeurs du Conservatoire National des Arts et Métiers: Dictionnaire biographique, 1974-1955.* Paris: Institut national de recherche pédagogique, 1994.

Foucault, Michel. *The Birth of the Clinic: An Archaeology of Medical Perception.* Alan Sheridan, trans. New York: Vintage Books, 1975.

———. *Discipline and Punish: The Birth of the Prison.* Alan Sheridan, trans. New York: Vintage Books, 1979.

———. *The History of Sexuality, vol. 1: An Introduction.* Robert Hurley, trans. New York: Vintage Books, 1980.

———. *The Care of the Self.* Robert Hurley, trans. New York: Vintage Books, 1988.

———. *The Use of Pleasure.* Robert Hurley, trans. New York: Vintage Books, 1990.

———. *Power: The Essential Works of Foucault, 1954-1984.* Robert Hurley et al., trans. New York: The New Press, 2000.

———. *"Society Must Be Defended": Lectures at the Collège de France, 1975-1976.* Mauro Bertani and Alessandro Fontana, eds. David Macey, trans. New York: Picador, 2003.

———. *Security, Territory, Population: Lectures at the Collège de France, 1977-1978.* Michel Senellart, ed. Graham Burchell, trans. London: Palgrave MacMillan, 2007.

Frey, Jean-Pierre. *La ville industrielle et ses urbanités: la distinction ouvrier-employé. Le Creusot. 1870–1930.* Bruxelles: P. Mardaga, 1986.

Fullbrook, Edward, ed. *Real World Economics: A Post-Autistic Economics Reader.* London: Anthem Press, 2006.

Girard, Louis. *Les libéraux français, 1814–1875.* Paris: Aubier, 1985.

Goldstein, Jan. *Console and Classify: The French Psychiatric Profession in the Nineteenth Century.* Cambridge: Cambridge University Press, 1987.

———. "Foucault among the Sociologists: The "Disciplines" and the History of the Professions." *History and Theory* 23, no. 2 (1984): 170–192.

Gordon, Colin, ed. *Power/Knowledge: Selected Interviews and Other Writings, 1972–1977.* New York: Pantheon Books, 1980.

Griveau, Léon. *Le charbon, le fer: un exemple de concentration industrielle au dix-neuvième siècle, 1835–1914.* Le Creusot: Écomusée du Creusot, 1977.

Guerrand, Roger-Henri. *Les origines du logement social en France.* Paris: Les Éditions ouvrières, 1967.

Gueslin, André. *L'invention de l'économie sociale: le dix-neuvième siècle français.* Paris: Economica, 1987.

Hauser, H. *L'enseignement des sciences sociales: État actuel de cet enseignement dans les divers pays du monde.* Paris: A. Chevalier-Maresq, 1903.

Hatzfeld, Henri. *Du paupérisme à la sécurité sociale: essai sur les origines de la sécurité sociale en France: 1850–1940.* Paris: Armand Colin, 1971.

Heilbroner, Robert L. *The Worldly Philosophers: The Lives, Times and Ideas of the Great Economic Thinkers.* New York: Simon and Schuster, 1961.

Herrenschmidt, Denise. "Les caisses de secours entre ouvriers à Mulhouse de 1800 à 1870." *Bulletin du Musée historique de Mulhouse* 66 (1958): 69–113.

Hildreth, Martha L. "The Balzac Revival in the Early Third Republic: Reconstructing the Doctor's Role in the Culture Wars over Science." Paper presented at the annual international meeting of the Western Society for French History, Lubbock, Texas, November 2004.

Hirschman, Albert O. *The Passions and the Interests: Political Arguments for Capitalism before its Triumph.* Princeton: Princeton University Press, 1977.

Horne, Janet R. *A Social Laboratory for Modern France: The Musée Social and the Rise of the Welfare State.* Durham: Duke University Press, 2002.

Jonas, Stephan, Philippe Heckner, and Jean-Michel Knorr. *La cité de Mulhouse, 1853-1870: un modèle d'habitat économique et social du dix-neuvième siècle.* Strasbourg: Association de recherche près l'Unité pédagogique d'architecture de Strasbourg, 1981.

Kahan-Rabecq, Marie-Madeleine. *L'Alsace économique et sociale sous le règne de Louis-Philippe.* Paris: Éditions des presses modernes, 1939.

Kott, Sandrine. "Enjeux et significations d'une politique sociale: la Société Industrielle de Mulhouse, 1827-1870." *Revue d'histoire moderne et contemporaine* (1987): 640-659.

———. "La Haute-Alsace: une région modèle en matière d'habitat ouvrier, 1853-1914." *La revue de l'économie sociale* (1988): 27-35.

———. "Des philanthropies aux politiques sociales: solutions françaises et allemandes à la questions sociale en Haute-Alsace, 1850-1914." Thèse de troisième cycle, Université de Paris VII, 1991.

La mine et les mineurs: groupe de recherche sur l'histoire du syndicalisme minier à Montceau-les-Mines, 1899-1950. Unpublished manuscript, Écomusée du Creusot, 1984.

Larrère, Catherine. *L'invention de l'économie au XVIIIè siècle: Du droit naturel à la physiocratie.* Paris: Presses universitaires de France, 1992.

Le Van-Lemesle, Lucette. *Le Juste ou le Riche: L'enseignement de l'économie politique, 1815-1950.* Paris: Comité pour l'histoire économique et financière de la France, 2004.

———. "Guillaumin, Éditeur d'économie politique, 1801-64." *Revue d'économie politique* 2 (1985): 134-49.

———. "La promotion de l'économie politique en France au dix-neuvième siècle jusqu'à son introduction dans les facultés, 1815-1881." *Revue d'histoire moderne et contemporaine* 27 (April-June 1980): 270-294.

Livet, Georges, and Raymond Oberlé. *Histoire de Mulhouse des origines à nos jours.* Strasbourg: Istra, 1977.

Lutfalla, Michel. "Aux origines du libéralisme économique en France: le *Journal des économistes*, analyse du contenu de la première série, 1841-1853." *Revue d'histoire économique et sociale* 4 (1972): 494–517.

Lynch, Katherine A. *Family, Class, and Ideology in Early Industrial France: Social Policy and the Working-Class Family, 1825-1848.* Madison: University of Wisconsin Press, 1988.

Marco, Luc, and Evelyne Laurent. *Le Journal des économistes, 1841-1940.* Paris: Éditions de l'Association Nationale des Docteur ès Sciences Économiques, 1990.

Melucci, Alberto. "Idéologies et pratiques patronales pendant l'industrialisation capitaliste: le cas de la France." Thèse de troisième cycle, École pratique des hautes études, 1974.

———. "Action patronale, pouvoir, organisation: Règlements d'usine et contrôle de la main-d'oeuvre au XIXe siècle." *Le mouvement social* 97 (1976): 139–59.

Monaghan, Peter. "Taking on 'Rational Man': Dissident Economists Fight for a Niche in the Discipline." *Chronicle of Higher Education* (January 24, 2003), http://chronicle.com/weekly/v49/i20/20a01201.htm.

Murard, Lion, and Patrick Zylberman. *Le petit travailleur infatigable, ou le prolétaire régénéré: Villes-usines, habitat et intimités au dix-neuvième siècle.* Paris: Recherches, 1976.

Noiriel, Gerard. "Espace de production et luttes sociales: l'exemple des usines sidérugiques lorraines, 1880–1930." *Le mouvement social* 125 (1983): 25–56.

———. *Les ouvriers dans la société française.* Paris: Éditions du Seuil, 1986.

———. "Du 'patronage' au 'paternalisme': la restructuration des formes de domination de la main d'oeuvre ouvrière dans l'industrie métallurgique française." *Le mouvement social* 144 (1988): 17–35.

Oberlé, Raymond. *L'enseignement à Mulhouse de 1798 à 1870.* Strasbourg: Faculté des lettres de l'Université de Strasbourg, 1961.

Parize, René. "La stratégie patronale au Creusot pendant les grèves de 1899–1900." *Cahiers d'histoire de l'Institut Maurice Thorez* 24 (1978): 13–46.

———. "Le paternalisme et son influence politique au Creusot de 1899 à 1939." Thèse de troisième cycle, Université de Toulouse, 1980.

Perrot, Jean-Claude. *Une historie intellectuelle de l'économie politique, XVII-XVIII siècle.* Paris: Éditions de l'École des Hautes Études en Sciences Sociales, 1992.

Perrot, Michelle. "The Three Ages of Industrial Discipline in Nineteenth-Century France." John M. Merriman, ed. *Consciousness and Class Experience in Nineteenth-Century Europe*. New York: Holmes and Meier, 1979.

Pirou, Gaetan. *Les doctrines économiques en France depuis 1870*. Paris: A. Colin, 1952.

Pollard, Sidney. "Factory Discipline in the Industrial Revolution." *Economic History Review* 16 (1963): 254–71.

———. *The Genesis of Modern Management*. Cambridge: Harvard University Press, 1965.

Procacci, Giovanna. *Gouverner la Misère: la Question Sociale en France, 1789–1848*. Paris: Éditions Seuil, 1993.

———. "Governing Poverty: Sources of the Social Question in Nineteenth-Century France." Jan Goldstein, ed. *Foucault and the Writing of History*. Cambridge: Basil Blackwell Ltd., 1994.

Ransom, John S. *Foucault's Discipline: The Politics of Subjectivity*. Durham: Duke University Press, 1997.

Rébérioux, Madeleine. "Naissance de l'économie sociale." *La Revue de l'économie sociale* 1 (1984): 9–15.

Reid, Donald. "Industrial Paternalism: Discourse and Practice in Nineteenth-Century French Mining and Metallurgy." *Comparative Studies in Society and History* 27 (1985): 579–607.

———. "The Origins of Industrial Labor Management in France: The Case of the Decazeville Ironworks during the July Monarchy." *Business History Review* 57 (1985): 1–19.

———. "Labour Management and Labour Conflict in Rural France: the Aubin Miners' Strike of 1869." *Social History* 13 (1988): 25–44.

Rothschild, Emma. *Economic Sentiments: Adam Smith, Condorcet, and the Enlightenment*. Cambridge: Harvard University Press, 2001.

Scott, Joan Wallach. "'L'ouvrière! Mot impie, sordide...': Women Workers in the Discourse of French Political Economy, 1840–1860." *Gender and the Politics of History*. New York: Columbia University Press, 1988.

Shapiro, Ann-Louise. *Breaking the Codes: Female Criminality in Fin-de-Siècle Paris*. Stanford: Stanford University Press, 1996.

Staum, Martin S. "The Institute economists: from Physiocracy to entrepreneurial capitalism." *History of Political Economy* 19, no. 4 (Winter 1987): 525–50.

Stearns, Peter. *Paths to Authority: The Middle Class and the Industrial Labor Force in France, 1820–1848.* Urbana: University of Illinois Press, 1978.

Sutet, Marcel, and Jean-Pierre Brésillon. *Du terroir à l'usine: Le Creusot, Montceau-les-Mines autrefois.* Le Coteau: Horvath, 1983.

Topalov, Christian, ed. *Laboratoires du nouveau siècle: La nébuleuse réformatrice et ses réseaux en France, 1880–1914.* Paris: Éditions de l'École des hautes études en sciences sociales, 1999.

Troche, J.P. "Schneiderville/Le Creusot et la Cité du Charbon/Montceau-les-Mines: espace industriel, ville, habitat." Unpublished mémoire, Écomusée du Creusot, 1976.

Ventre-Denis, Madeleine. "Sciences sociales et université au dix-neuvième siècle: une tentative d'enseignement de l'économie politique à Paris sous la Restauration." *Revue historique* 520 (1976): 321–342.

Vitoux, Marie-Claire. *Paupérisme et assistance à Mulhouse au dix-neuvième siècle.* Strasbourg: Association des publications près les Universités de Strasbourg, 1986.

Weisz, George. *The Emergence of Modern Universities in France, 1863–1914.* Princeton: Princeton University Press, 1983.

———. "L'idéologie républicaine et les sciences sociales: les durkheimiens et la chaire d'histoire d'économie sociale à la Sorbonne." *Revue française de sociologie* 20 (1979): 83–112.

Whatmore, Richard. *Republicanism and the French Revolution: An Intellectual History of Jean-Baptiste Say's Political Economy.* Oxford: Oxford University Press, 2000.

Index

Studies in Modern European History

The monographs in this series focus upon aspects of the political, social, economic, cultural, and religious history of Europe from the Renaissance to the present. Emphasis is placed on the states of Western Europe, especially Great Britain, France, Italy, and Germany. While some of the volumes treat internal developments, others deal with movements such as liberalism, socialism, and industrialization, which transcend a particular country.

The series editor is:

Frank J. Coppa
Director, Doctor of Arts Program
in Modern World History
Department of History
St. John's University
Jamaica, New York 11439